Remembering My Life in the Hills of Kentucky

Remembering My Life in the Hills of Kentucky

Bertha Lee

authorHOUSE®

AuthorHouse™ LLC
1663 Liberty Drive
Bloomington, IN 47403
www.authorhouse.com
Phone: 1-800-839-8640

Published by AuthorHouse 06/05/2014

ISBN: 978-1-4969-1711-9 (sc)
ISBN: 978-1-4969-1710-2 (e)

Library of Congress Control Number: 2014909992

Contents

Chapter 1   I Remember 1

Chapter 2   Coming for to Carry me Home 10

Chapter 3   Gale Hollow 26

Chapter 4   Worst Times 40

Chapter 5   The Train Ride 48

Chapter 6   Hell Fire & Brimstone 59

Chapter 7   She'll be Coming 'Round the Mountain 76

Chapter 8   Thank God for Grandmas 85

Chapter 9   The End of Time 103

Chapter 10   Back to Indiana 115

Chapter 1

I Remember

My first memory was of arms grabbing wildly for me. I remember Mommy was holding me on her hip. She kind of stuck her hip out and I sat on it like riding a horse. She held on to me with one arm and the other was free to do whatever she was doing at the time. I remember she bent over and put her free hand on a person's face that was lying down on a low bed. It was an old woman. When Mommy's hand touched her face she screamed and reached both her arms toward me. That was my nightmare. I seemed to not be able to get that out of my head. I can remember waking up at night with that image in my head for the longest time. When I was older and could talk, I told my Mommy about what scared me so bad. She said I was walking at the time and an old lady who lived near by was dying and she had gone over to sit up with her, which was the custom in those days. She didn't give it a thought that I would be aware of what was going on but the old lady died or so they thought. Since Mommy had some knowledge of what to do at those times, she bent over to close her eyes. When she put her hand on the lady's face to close her eyes, the lady screamed and reached her arms up toward Mommy and me. Mommy said she lived three more days before she finally died but I was hysterical for a long time. I think soon after that my little brother Bill was born. After Bill came to live with us I didn't dream that bad dream so much. Mommy must have been pregnant when that lady died.

Johnie was my older brother. He was named after Daddy's brother John and Mommy's brother Henry. Everyone had two names back then and sometimes more. There was a song called John Henry the Steel Driving Man and Daddy would sing that a lot to Johnie. It would make him so mad. Johnie was always following Daddy around if he could.

Bill was named after Daddy's brother Bill and Mommy's brother Adam. I have a clear memory of Bill taking his first steps. We were eating supper and Mommy cleared the table. She stood Bill on one end of the table and he walked across the table to Daddy. We all clapped and Johnie and I clapped for a long time. For a while after that it seemed Bill walked on the table at every meal. Bill got better at walking. He could walk all over without falling down. I tell you he was the busiest little fellow and to this day he hasn't changed a bit.

Our little house was just that, little. There were only two rooms, a kitchen and an all-purpose room you could call it I guess. We slept in that room and spent our evenings there. If we had company we visited there also. Mommy sewed and quilted, while we played games and read. Sometimes we cooked over the open fireplace in the cold weather and ate there too. There was one window and an outside door in each room.

Bill seldom got the run of the house because he was fast for a little guy. Mommy would put a chair across the door between the kitchen and the front room to stop him. She would lay the kitchen chair down on its side and it blocked the doorway pretty good. I remember Johnie and I were in the yard playing and some how little little busy body Bill got around the chair and into the kitchen. The outside door was open and Bill just ran right out the door. It was high off the ground and there were three big flat rocks for steps and he hit them all. Johnie and I were screaming our heads off. Mommy jumped out the door and never touched a step. She bent down over Bill, I thought she was biting him but she was blowing in his mouth. After a little while he began to cry. Boy my Mommy knew a lot of things. They said she breathed life into him. I remember thinking at the time; I'm not ever going to walk out of that door.

There were things I remember so clearly even though I was very young. We were always gathering things for the winter. At that time you could pick wild berries and greens. There were plum and apple trees growing right out along the road or the edge of the woods. There were persimmons and papaws. There were all kinds of nut trees, walnuts, hazelnuts, hickory, and chestnuts. There were huge beech trees and there were nuts on them. We gathered them all. Mommy and Daddy raised a big garden and worked very hard putting things up for the winter.

Picking berries were always the hottest and hardest gathering that we did. Not only was it hard work we usually got chiggers too. We all went on those trips. Daddy took the sled and all the buckets we could find. The mule pulled the sled and us kids. It seemed as if the good things were always on a hill or some place that was hard to reach. They put the sled under a tree and Bill and I stayed in the sled. Johnie ran around pretending to help. We were there all day that day. You could look down the hill and in the valley was the store and the house the storekeeper lived in. I guess he was rich because he had a saw mill up the hollow behind the store. He owned some houses he rented to people also.

We lived in one of those houses as did Mommy's friends Betsy, Deb and their kids. Some times they visited us and we visited with them. It was getting late that day and we were getting ready to go home when Daddy said, "Look Charity, what are they doing at the store," so we all watched. Men were running around with sticks poking around under stacks of lumber, which was in the store yard. You could see it plain as anything. Deb bent over and poked his stick into the lumber pile and Kane the storeowner had a gun. He put the gun right against Deb's head and shot him. It was awful. We all cried and Daddy said, "We better go help." Mommy said, "No, we don't know what was going on. We'll take the berries home and work them up. Then we'll go see what we can do." So that's what we did.

I talked to Mommy about it after I was older. She said Kane had a teenaged daughter who always did the milking, and the summer before the cows had got out. Deb worked at the saw mill for Kane, so Kane sent him down to help her get the cows into the barn. Deb had a shotgun with him, which was normal in those days. Almost everyone carried a gun of some kind. He sat the gun in the barn while they got the cows up, and the little girl knocked the gun over and it went off and killed her. Mommy always thought that was why Kane killed Deb. Kane said he was killing rats, but only one shot was fired and everyone saw him put the gun against Deb's head. So Kane was taken away to prison and his family sold the store, saw mill, and all the houses.

I remember Deb's funeral, everyone cried so hard. Mommy took food and clothes to Betsy and the kids. Betsy moved away right after the funeral.

It wasn't long after Deb was killed that school started. Johnie went to school but I wasn't old enough. Every now and then Mommy would let me go visit school. I thought that was just about the best thing that could possibly happen and would beg to go everyday. The older girls would play with me, comb my hair and teach me to write and make numbers. They gave me all kinds of things like paper, broken crayons and little short pencils. Those were treasures to me.

School and learning was very important to my mother. She wanted us children to learn everything we could. Everyday I went to school I had to tell her what all happened. If I learned a word or how to draw or write a number she would brag about it to anyone who would listen. We got a grit paper every week and we had a Bible. Mommy sewed for the schoolteacher who gave her magazines and schoolbooks with the backs tore off and pages torn or missing. We wore those books and magazines out.

I begged so hard to go to school that Mommy said I could go some days but the day I failed to learn something I couldn't go until I was six. When you are four years old six seemed like a long time away. I was sure to learn something everyday.

The people who bought the house we lived in from Kane's family wanted us to move but Daddy talked to them and they let us stay until school was out.

One day Johnie and I were walking home from school and we met the midwife. Everyone knew her. She said, "I just come from your house and I left you a little baby boy. He is so little you can hardly see him." I was so happy and Johnie asked her where she found him. She said, "Right here," and she patted her saddlebags real hard. I remember thinking; I hope there isn't another baby in there because she'll hurt it. She said, "I just look in there and sometimes there's a baby and I take it to someone I know wants a baby. Your mommy has brought me a couple of babies so I owed her." She said she would be back tomorrow and rode off on her horse.

We ran home as fast as we could. He was such a little tiny baby and Mommy wouldn't let us hold him. She kept him on a feather pillow with a pretty soft blanket over him and wrapped up real good. They named him Hiram Thomas after my mother's Uncle Tom and Daddy's grandpa Hiram. Daddy said the baby wasn't any bigger than two toots, so he was called Toots. For a long time when anyone except Mommy held toots they would hold pillow and all. I didn't fuss to go with Johnie to school nearly as much after the baby came.

I can remember crawling up on the bed and just lying there beside the pillow that held my own little baby and watching him for hours. When anyone asked about the baby they would refer to him as my baby. I was so proud of him. Mommy wouldn't let the boys get on the bed with him and I saw to it that they didn't. I watched him like a hawk. I would scream my head off if anyone even acted like they were going to touch him. I can't describe how I felt about that little fellow. I knew I loved him better than anyone.

That year at Christmas I went to school with Johnie. The day they had the play I sang a song. I remember it so well. Daddy taught me the words. Daddy made banjos out of cans that hams came in. He used copper wire and some kind of wood. Back then times were really hard but we had a new president and he was trying to do things for the CCCS. It was called Civilian Conservation Corps. It was kind of like an army but they didn't fight, they built parks and ponds and planted trees and sewed grass. They worked all over doing good things for the country and were paid for it. They got free clothes, a place to stay, and good food to eat. Most of them sent their money home to their families.

The older men with families worked at building roads. There were no gravel roads in that part of the country and a lot of places just had footpaths. They call that operation the W.P.A., and that stood for, Work Projects Administration. Everyone who worked for the W.P.A. got paid and sometimes they would get heavy coats and shoes and whatever clothes they needed for their jobs because they were always out in the weather. Sometimes they got hams in tin cans and bags of beans and sugar, and a lot of other things. Daddy made our banjos out of those ham cans. Johnie, Bill and I would pick those homemade banjos to pieces. We sang too. I think it would be such a great thing if we could have had a movie of us kids playing them ham can banjos and just singing our little heads off. Mommy and Daddy sang right along with us and acted like we were just the best singers you ever heard.

Mommy made all our clothes. Back then the churches had rummage sales. Our preacher was from Michigan and had friends there who sent big boxes of clothing on the train to our church. Some of the men would take their wagons and bring them to the church. The women would help put them out and run the sales. They would get to pick out what they wanted for free. Mommy always helped. She would pick out the biggest things with the best material. I'll always remember those big riding skirts. She would rip them up and make us clothes out of them.

Almost every year we had a flood or sometime two in the mountains. Everyone was used to it and I remember just before school was out we had one that wasn't really expected right then. I had gone to school with Johnie that day. It had rained the day before and I remember Mommy and Daddy talking about whether or not we should go to school. It wasn't raining right then so we went to school. The schoolhouse was on the other side of the creek. We had to cross a swinging bridge. If there wasn't a flood you could walk across the creek if you didn't care about getting your feet wet. That day the water was up and after we were at school it began to rain again and by lunch mothers and dads had begun to come to get their kids. The water was out of the banks and almost touching the swinging bridge. Men brought their horses and mules. They would take us from dry ground to the bridge and some one would be waiting to take us from the bridge to dry ground to the other side. That was scary but exciting and we would have something to talk about for quite some time. School was out shortly after the flood and Daddy had found a place for us to move to but it was a lot farther from school and Mommy worried about us walking so far in the wintertime.

Daddy had taken us to see where we were moving and we loved it but when the moving day came it was sad for us kids. I guess it was hard for Mommy and Daddy to move all the animals and other stuff but Daddy got his brother-in-law and nephews to help us. Mommy took us kids to her friend Betsy. She kept us until the moving was done. Betsy had found a new husband and he was very nice. But they had moved in with an old man who was very sick and had no family to care for him. He gave his house and everything he owned to Betsy and Carter if they would look after him the rest of his life. I was scared of him for no reason. He wasn't mean or anything and I don't know why I was scared. We weren't there long just a couple of days but while we were there the old man had a bad spell and he hemorrhaged real bad. That was part of his sickness. It sure was hard on us kids to see that. Blood came out of his mouth and nose and just got all over the bed. I cried so hard. I was afraid I would catch what he had. I stood in the doorway and tried to keep Johnie and Bill from going in. Betsy made her older girl, Ora Mae, take us into another room. We were so glad when Mommy and Daddy came to get us. The old man died soon after that but I never wanted to go back to Betsy's and cried when they took us to visit. The boys weren't bothered by it at all.

When Daddy and Mommy came to get us they brought the sled, the old mule, and the pony also. Carter and Daddy had done some trading. Daddy got some tools and other things and Mommy and Daddy were going to make the coffin for the old man when he died. Back then people didn't have much money so they traded a lot and they gave their word and shook hands on a trade. Now it takes several pounds of paper and a lawyer or two to make a trade.

We didn't have to keep toots on the pillow anymore but I guess he got used to it because if he didn't have it he would have a crying fit. We all had feather pillows. We had geese and an old mean gander that hated me and chased me a lot. Mommy helped our neighbor pick geese and they paid her with an old goose, a dozen geese eggs and that old mean gander. When the eggs hatched out she had a dozen geese. She would pick the geese when they were ready to shed and saved the feathers. She would take her little short pealing chair outside and take the goose's head in the bend of her leg and pick that goose in a minute. The geese looked funny for a few days but soon the feathers would grow back and they were just fine again. My mommy was so smart. She knew a lot of things and we all had soft feather pillows.

Mommy had brought a tub with covers in it and she put toots and his pillow in that and I rode in the sled with him. Johnie and Bill rode the pony and Mommy and Daddy walked along beside the sled. We headed out to our new home and it was a good happy time.

Jim & Charity

Chapter 2

Coming for to Carry me Home

I remember watching my mother and father as they selected just the right stones from the branch in back of the house for the walk. It was spring and they carried the rocks in a sled to the yard. I can see them placing the stones as we laughed and it seemed we were all children, not working but playing some sort of a game.

We waited eagerly for the rain after the walk was laid and when it had rained enough to soak the earth. Mommy, Daddy, my brothers, and I walked on the stones until they were embedded in the ground.

Daddy whistled and sang a lot. People called him whistling Jim. Mommy's name was Charity, and Daddy would sing, "Swing Low Sweet Charity," to her. I don't remember how old I was when I finally discovered the word was really Chariot.

There was a ridge near by were the nut trees grew. Daddy would put sideboards on the sled while Mommy gathered the coffee sacks. Because the hill was so steep we had to travel around the hill to get to the top but it was a real treat once the top was reached.

You could see forever on that ridge. We played a game we called Cover up. You put your hand out as far as you could reach, then count the places you had covered. It was like lying you hand on a map. As small as my hand was I covered the South Fork of Goose Creek, the saw mill and Joe Buck's house and barn, all in one cover up.

While we were playing and we let the baby wander near the chestnut tree. Mommy had put my older brother and me in charge of the two younger boys. At that time they were four and two years old. Johnie was eight and I was six. I ran to get the baby. We all feared Mommy's wrath. She was the stronger of our parents. She made most of the decisions and if punishment was needed she took care of that too.

Daddy was up in the chestnut tree and I grabbed the baby and looked up. Just as I looked up a chestnut fell hitting me in the eye. It was hard for me to know what was happening. I felt as if a fire was inside my head and I screamed as I held my hands over my eyes. They boys were crying too.

Mommy and daddy were trying to look into my eyes to see how bad I was hurt. They wet one of the baby's diapers and tied it around my head and eyes. All the time Mommy was giving orders. She said, "Take her to Doctor Wally as fast as you can!" Then she yelled at Johnie to run ahead and get the pony ready!

Daddy was already running down the hill with me in his arms. Mommy was yelling after him, "Stop at Billy's and have him take you the rest of the way and I'll follow you." The last thing I heard her say was, "For God's sake hurry!"

Daddy never stopped running. I could tell we were going down hill because he stumbled and fell and part of the time he sat down and slid. There was a smooth path after we were down the hill and he was running fast with Johnie running a little way ahead. We were going down the hollow now and it was cool and shaded and I could hear the water running in the branch beside the path. We came out of the woods a good way from the barn. I felt the warm sun and I knew where we were.

Daddy said, "Forget about the saddle, just put the bridle on." We got on the pony while Daddy was telling Johnie to go back up the hollow and help Mommy.

The pony ran fast at first then it began to get slower and slower. Daddy just got off and hit the pony and said, "Go home." He began to run again. He never stopped until he got to Billy Dee's house. He got into the Model T Ford and leaned on the horn until Billy came out. When he seen what a sad state we were in he took us the rest of the way. The road was a dirt road and a rough trip that seemed to take forever.

I expected Doctor Wally to cure me instantly and make all the pain go away. Instead he closed his office and began to try to examine me. I held onto Daddy and the Doctor said, "I can't help her, I can't tell how bad it is. We've got to get her to Lexington soon."

He put big pieces of bandages over my eyes and wrapped cloth all around my head. By this time I was throwing up and I could hear the pounding inside my head. The doctor's office was in his house and I can still hear his booming voice, "Mrs. Wally I need you."

In a second she was there. I remember thinking, the doctor reminds me of Mommy. He began giving orders, talking loud and fast. I supposed she was writing as he talked. He said, "Call Bledso and tell him to get the car ready, we're going to Lexington within the hour. Call the hospital there and tell them to get ready for us. We'll be there around daybreak. We've got an eye injury."

He called Daddy by his name like they were old friends or relatives. "Jim you'll have to ride with us. Daddy was holding me and trying to clean the vomit from me with a cloth. I was snubbing and I could feel Daddy's chest and it was heaving. He was having a hard time getting his breath. He tried to lay me down on a big chair but I wouldn't let go of him and he sat down and cried while Cassie, Doctor Wally's wife, cleaned us up the best she could.

There was a lot of noise outside and I heard Mommy's voice. It never occurred to me that I would be able to recognize a voice or feel a presence and know who it was without seeing. I knew my brothers were there, even though none of them spoke. I could hear the baby breathing the same way Daddy did, wheezy and rattling, and the flap, flapping of Johnie's shoe sole that was loose, and he kept throwing his foot out so the sole wouldn't fold back under his foot as he walked. Bill always sniffled his nose and today he was sniffing and little faster and harder than usual.

Mommy ran to the big chair and lifted me into her arms and I never knew if it was the shot Doctor Wally had given me or her comforting touch that caused me to sleep, but when I woke we were somewhere between Manchester and Lexington. The car was big and it had soft seats like the chair at Doctor Wally's house. Mommy and I sat on one seat and Daddy sat on the other with the Doctor. It was a strange car. The driver sat up front by himself and the doctor opened a window between us to talk to him. The window kept getting stuck and Doctor Wally would pound on the window and cuss at it.

Daddy had fallen asleep and we could hear his heavy labored breathing. Doctor Wally said, "Charity, we've got to do something about Jim's asthma."

It was still night when we arrived at the hospital. There were people everywhere. Daddy carried me inside and I was put on a table with people swarming all around. All the time the strangers were examining me Doctor Wally held onto my hand. I had begun to trust him.

A decision was made because unfamiliar hands began to undress me and the fight began. I kicked and screamed. I even bit someone. Someone else said, "What hollow did you trap this little wildcat in?" They all laughed and Doctor Wally yelled, "You're making jokes, while this little girl is going blind." You could have heard him all the way to

Manchester. I loved him then almost as much as I loved Daddy. He picked me up and carried me into the operating room and placed me carefully on the table, patted me on the arm and walked away.

The next thing I felt was something cold on my face, shaped like a bowl and the strange voice said, "This won't hurt a bit, it'll feel good." And being the little wildcat they said I was, I came back with, "If it feels so damn good put it on you own face." The last thing I heard was Doctor Wally's booming laugh. I had said something to make him laugh and I was happy.

When I woke up everything was different. All around were sounds of children crying, some talking, some crying "nurse, nurse," and some calling mommy. I was one of those. I couldn't stop throwing up and my head was pounding and bandaged up. Of course I still couldn't see.

Before long Mommy and Daddy came in. I thought they were coming to take me home, but instead Mommy was the one to tell me. She said, "You have been so good and now you have got to be brave because you're going to have to stay here for a while so you can see again."

I was crying again and I told her I didn't care if I could see, I wanted to go home now. Then she told me that she cared and Daddy cared. "Now you stay here and get well or you'll answer to me." She bent over and kissed my hands and face and her face was wet. Daddy hugged and kissed me and they left. I was all alone.

The days were a hundred years long and I stopped crying. I listened to the other children crying and wondered what was wrong with them. Close to my bed was a baby who cried all the time. They cry got weaker each day and sometime in the night the crying stopped and the next day a new voice was crying in the bed beside me.

I stayed sick and threw up for a long time. I couldn't eat and I wouldn't talk but I didn't cry anymore. The nurses forced food down me. I hated everyone. I wanted to be back in the big room in the mountains where my family was laughing and making work seem like play. I hungered for my brothers and wondered if I would ever be able to go home.

A lot of people came to the hospital to visit the children. I could tell when the mothers and fathers stopped to stare at the pitiful little mountain girl who had no visitors and a mean nasty way about her.

There was nothing to do but travel back in my mind to the mountains and the family I loved so much. One of my trips was interrupted when I heard a voice say, "How are you? My name is Miss Linda. Can I get you anything? A drink, ice cream, or maybe I can read for you." I still wasn't talking so I turned over with my back to her and she sat down beside my bed and began to read, "Alice in Wonderland."

Mommy used to read the grit paper to us, and sometimes the schoolteacher who lived up the road from us gave us books with colored pictures in them. There were all kinds of pictures of pretty houses.

Our house was very old and was made out of logs. The big room had one window and in the winter Mommy hung a quilt over it to keep the cold out. The fireplace was so big all four of us kids could get in it and there was room for four more and a couple of dogs. The hearth was one big stone that had been chipped away to make it kind of square. It wasn't smooth but had nice little humps and valleys that you could lay a nut in and it wouldn't roll away. We always kept a stack of nice shaped cracking rocks on the hearth.

There were two big iron beds in the room. Mommy and Daddy slept in one and the boys in the other. My bed was made from dynamite boxes Daddy brought from the mines. There was only enough room for one small person. There was a shuck tick for a mattress. The bed sat over in the corner by the fireplace.

The best night was Saturday. That was when the grit paper came, a big boy, bigger than Johnie brought it. His name was Bad Eye Sandlin. He had one eye. No one ever talked about what happened to his eye and I never knew what his real name was. He carried his shoes in the big canvas bag along with the papers. He never wore them until ice froze on the puddles in the road. He collected the dimes for the paper and put them in a red Prince Albert can that had Bad Eye scratched on the front.

After supper was over on Saturday and the work was done we all got in the same bed, Mommy, Daddy, my three brothers and me. Mommy would then read the grit to us. We laughed at the funny stories and cried at the sad ones. Usually we kids fell asleep and Mommy and Daddy would slip out leaving us to sleep out the night in their bed.

The nice lady stopped reading. She said, "I must go but I'll be back tomorrow." Sure enough she came back, sat down and began to read from the same book. This time I listened to her. But before she left she got a bowl of ice cream. She didn't try to make me eat, but she put the back of the spoon in the ice cream and rubbed it against my lips. It sure tasted good. Back home we had snow cream in the winter but it didn't taste as good as this. Every day she came and repeated that same ritual, the reading, and then the ice cream.

One morning she came earlier than usual, I always knew when she came into the room. For just a second the room would get very quite and there would be a swishing sound of her dress that was different from the nurses and she smelled different too. No one else in the whole world smelled like Miss Linda.

I was in a baby bed with the side rails up. It was like jail and I didn't want to get out. It was my world now. Miss Linda put the rail down and set me up. I did whatever she wanted. Today she wanted me to eat. She said, "This is oatmeal. Have you ever eaten oats?" I shook my head no. She said, "I eat this every morning for breakfast. It's the best food in the world." She fed the oats to me and I ate it all without a fight. The ward was quite. They were watching the taming of the little wildcat.

My new friend came to visit every day. She began taking me out of the bed and holding me on her lap when she read to me. The nurses were pleased with this new development because I had fought them so much. They left me to Miss Linda and that suited me just fine.

I still wasn't talking to anyone, not even Miss Linda. I heard the nurse ask the doctor if they took my tongue out. I thought, she'll never know.

I didn't know how many children were in the room but there were a lot. I would try to count the different sounding voices, but it was useless because the voices kept changing all the time, and most of the time someone was crying, even when the gift people came through. They gave me gifts at first but they stopped. I could hear them come through and they just passed me by. I thought it was because I was so mean and wouldn't eat or talk. I found out later it was because I wanted everything in the bed where I could touch them. I ran out of room so they put my things in a box. When some one I wasn't familiar with came by I'd gather all my treasures into my arms and hold them. I spent a lot of time like that.

I didn't know how long I had been there in the hospital but when I came there we were going bare foot, now the doctors and nurses were talking about snow and how cold it was outside. Mommies and Daddies were talking about Christmas, Santa, and presents. I still wasn't talking about anything, but I began to make plans. I knew Santa went everywhere in the world so when he came here I would talk to him and maybe he would take me to Manchester and to my home.

Miss Linda came before Santa. Long before she got to my bed I was reaching for her. This day she picked me up and said, Little Kitten, how would you like to go home with me?" Miss Linda always called me Little

Kitten. I hugged her tight and broke my long silence. So no one could hear, I put my mouth right on her ear and whispered very low, "I want to go to my Mommy and Daddy's house," and I cried.

She carried me around through the ward, back and forth like you would a baby with the colic. When I stopped crying she sat down and told me why I couldn't go home. She said, "Everyday for a long time you will have to come back here to the hospital, so the doctors can treat your eyes. You will have to be watched very closely. Now its home with me or stay here." Once again I put my mouth up to her ear and whispered very low, "I love you." She picked me up and danced through the ward holding me close.

The next day the bandages came off. Miss Linda was there and I could hear the nurses hushing the children and it was the first time the room had been that quiet since I had been there. Miss Linda was holding my hand. I could hear the curtains being closed. The babies weren't crying and the only noise was people breathing. They carefully unwrapped the bandages and removed the big pieces of gauze. I was afraid to open my eyes but even before I opened them I knew I could see. A little light came through.

I could only open one eye and the first thing I saw was my friend. She was beautiful. She was taller than my mother and older. Her hair was more gray than brown and she looked like the pretty ladies in the Ladies Home Journal. Maybe I had really died and this was Heaven and maybe the tall lady was Jesus. Of course that couldn't be right, because everyone in Heaven was well and no one in this place was well.

I was standing in the bed now, turning around and around. The room was huge and lined up on both sides were baby beds. Some had babies in them, but every child that had legs and could stand was crowded around my bed. The nurses were there, each holding a baby. There were doctors and they were all looking at me, some were smiling and others were crying. My friend took me out of the bed and put me on the floor. My gown was too long but I held it up and walked all through the ward looking at all the things I had listened to for so long.

I had new clothes Miss Linda had brought for me to wear. Fancy things like I had never seen before. Leggings and coat all the same color and a hat with lace on it. We went out into the city. I had seen pictures in the Ladies Home Journal like this but they couldn't compare with this. All the sounds, the flashing lights and store windows were enough to make a little mountain girl speechless again. I just stood there very still, looking and listening.

My friend threw back her head and laughed out loud, as if she had a magic wand, she waved her hand around in a circle and a car appeared right in front of us. I watched as a nice dressed man got out and held the car door open for Miss Linda. He then turned toward and bowed low to me, while he pointed to the open door of the big car.

My friend was still laughing as the driver loaded my treasures into the car. She leaned toward him and said, "Drive slowly; I want Little Kitten to see everything." I couldn't look at everything enough. Christmas was near and the city was dressed for it. I was talking fast, telling Miss Linda about all the things she saw everyday. When we got through the part of town and there were no more stores she said, "Turn around and drive through again."

It was almost dark when the big car pulled up in the driveway of the brick house. I thought it was another hospital and didn't want to get out. Miss Linda got out and said we're home and she picked me up and carried me into the house. The nice man followed with my treasures.

Just inside the door was a big open place with a huge light hanging from a shiny chain. It was sparkled like the sun shining on the trees after an ice storm back home. Only difference was the ice always melted after awhile and the light sparkled all the time. The floor was soft and

I wanted to walk in it barefoot. The wide stairs had the soft rug all the way up. We took our coats off and hung them in a little room made special for coats. There were hats on the shelf and lots of polished boots on the floor. Hanging on the door was silky scarves of every color one could imagine.

We went through two doors that were so big you could have driven a sled through without touching either side. I turned around and around looking while Miss Linda laughed. Windows from the floor to the ceiling were all around the room with curtains that felt like the weasel hide Daddy trapped back home, soft and dark like the night. The same soft rug was on the floor. There was a fireplace, but the hearth was smooth and you couldn't crack nuts on the hearth. They would roll away. There were a lot of soft chairs and two were so big I judge four grown ups could sit on one. In the middle of the room was a round table with one of those starry lights over it. A tan lace cloth that almost touched the floor was on the table. I never saw so many chairs in one place before.

That room was where I spent most of my time while I stayed at Miss Linda's. I took my shoes off and walked on the floor. It was the same light blue as the flowers that grew on the ridge in the spring. You could pull a string and close the curtains. It made the room dark in the daytime so the lights had to be turned on.

By this time I had attracted quite an audience. There were two older girls, almost as tall as Miss Linda. One had a patch on her eye, much like mine. There was an older lady wearing a white apron and holding a little fat baby girl. She was blind. Where its eyes should have been was sunken places. The lady put her down on the floor we crawled around on the floor together. I would call to her, "pretty baby," and she would come straight to me. We would hold onto each other and roll around on the floor laughing. We crawled under the table and holding onto each other until we fell asleep.

The next morning I woke in Miss Linda's bed. There were special little rooms everywhere, a room for clothes and a room to bathe. There was a room to sew and one to read in. Miss Linda lifted me into the tub of warm soapy water and I found out what made her smell so good. It was the soap. Mommy made our soap and it smelled bad. She called it lye ball soap. I hadn't thought about home now for a whole day and I began to feel guilty. I wandered what they were doing and I wished they could see this fancy place.

I was brought back to the present by the smell of hot oatmeal. She hadn't been teasing about the oatmeal. We had oats every morning for my whole stay at the big house in Lexington.

Time went fast at the big house. There were trips to the hospital almost daily. Some days we walked and the nice man took us if the weather was bad. We would stop at the stores and do something Miss Linda called shopping, but we never brought anything home with us. Back home when we went to the store we got lots of things. We would fill up two coffee sacks with goods. Daddy tied the sacks together and put them on the mule. We rode to the store and walked back. I found out later people brought the things to the back door in boxes and bags. It wasn't much fun shopping with Miss Linda.

Soon after I came to the big house, the tall girl with the patch got well and went home. The other girl stayed and went to school and parties. She dressed up in fancy dresses and furry coats. She came into the big room to show Miss Linda how pretty she was. She would turn round and round until her dress went way out and you could see her underwear. Sometimes she gave her lipstick and rouge to me and I would put it on my face. Miss Linda scolded her and washed my face.

My favorite time was when they brought pretty baby down to play each evening. We crawled all around the room and held onto each other and I pretended she was my brother.

I had collected a lot of treasures while I was there in Lexington and I kept them under the table. The table, like everything else at Lexington was big. It had one leg and four feet that looked like claws, each holding a glass ball. There was plenty of room for all my toys and enough left over for a little girl to hide and cry for her family. The lace tablecloth almost touched the floor making a nice little room and when the light was on it would shine through the cloth making everything under the table appear to be spotted.

It was close to Christmas and Miss Linda had visitors everyday. Everyone who came brought boxes or sacks of toys and clothing. They put them in another room in the back part of the house. That room had nothing in it except for the hundreds of boxes and sacks, which were stacked to the ceiling.

I had already decided this was where Santa stored presents for the whole world. Sometimes Miss Linda would bring some of the new toys and let me play with them. She would say, "Little Kitten, you must test this and see if it's fit for a six year old to play with." After I had tired of it she would bring out something else to be tested.

I was lonesome for my family and despite all Miss Linda's efforts I withdrew and spent more and more time under the big table. I named my paper dolls after my family back home.

Sometimes the kitchen lady came into the big room to tidy up. I knew right away she didn't like me because she would never smile and kept trying to move my stuff from under the table. Miss Linda talked to her real low but I heard them. Miss Linda wasn't smiling when she said, "I can do without you but Little Kitten stays." I never saw that kitchen lady again.

Now that Christmas was almost here, Miss Linda had company for supper a lot, but even when the extra chairs were used and the table was made bigger, she never once took my treasures from under the table. She had nice friends who were careful of my treasures and sometimes added to them.

It was the week of Christmas and I couldn't believe the tree. Miss Linda and I had red dresses that looked like gowns. We stood in front of the mirror in the big room and looked at ourselves. We hugged each other and giggled and I crawled under the table and told my paper doll family all about the pretty red dresses.

Miss Linda's friends helped put the shiny balls and icicles on the tree. Everyone who came brought a new shiny pretty for the tree and a treasure for pretty baby and me. The nurses brought a dress with a hat for me, just like they wore. The doctors sent a real doctor bag with a heart listener and real tape, bandages, and little wooden sticks. I had to use both hands to carry it and Miss Linda kept saying, "I can't believe they gave Little Kitten these things."

The best treasure came in the mail the next day. Miss Linda helped me unwrap it. There was a hat and gloves that matched. I knew Mommy had knitted them. Daddy had made a whistle from the cane poles that grew along the branch by the barn. Johnie sent his marbles. And Bill's wind up man was in the package. There was a family of corn shuck dolls. The clothes were made from scrapes left over from things Mommy had made for us. I couldn't play with them until I crawled up on Miss Linda's lap and cried.

Christmas Eve both my stockings were hung over the fireplace. It still didn't seem like Christmas to me. Christmas back home was different than here. Long before Christmas Mommy was making things for all of us. The sewing machine would go all day sometimes, and at night she knitted warm hats and gloves and long stockings for my brothers and me.

Daddy made whistles from cane poles. He made animals from nuts. He built pens and a shed from cane poles and a whole herd of pigs from acorns. Christmas lasted all winter long at our house in the mountains. We popped corn over the big open fireplace, and there was always a willow basket full of nuts sitting by the hearth. No one complained about the cracking rocks we kept on the hearth. We could crack as many nuts as we could eat. Cleaning up was easy. You just threw the hulls in the fire.

Mommy always began to tell the Christmas stories long before Christmas. She read the Jesus story without looking at the book.

At Miss Linda's house we sat around the big smooth hearth and watched the magic fire that never went out, never needed logs put on, or ashes taken out. The lady with the white apron came down and brought pretty baby. The tall party girl came down also. The new kitchen lady brought all kinds of cookies, candy, and nuts that were already cracked. There was a big bowl of boiled custard, but Miss Linda called it eggnog. It had nutmeg sprinkled on top and you could smell it all through the house.

After Christmas things got a little better for me. The bandages came off and a patch was put on my eye like a pirate. The people began to bring the boxes and the room began to fill up for next year.

It was on week before my birthday when the big car pulled up in front of Miss Linda's house and Doctor Wally got out. I ran to meet him and he threw me up in the air and hugged me. You could hear his booming voice all over as he carried me up the walk into the house. As soon as we were in the house he took out the little flashlight and began looking into my eyes. He kept nodding his head, repeating over and over again, looking good, looking good.

I was so excited about going home, I forgot about Miss Linda. She was standing over by the table with the cloth folded back. I began to cry. She got some boxes for me and I crawled under the table and packed my treasures, except for Johnie's marbles, Bill's wind up man and the little family of corn shuck dolls. I left them carefully placed on the table leg for the special lady who had taken such good care of the lonely, scared little mountain girl.

The car pulled away from the big house. The tall lady stood in the street and waved until the car was out of sight.

Chapter 3
Gale Hollow

As we pulled up to the house I can actually smell the smoke from the wood fire. It was so different from the oily, smoky city smells. I closed my eyes to listen to the quiet of the mountains.

Mommy had hired Mr. Tipps to bring me home in his wagon. He must have thought I was addled or touched as the mountain folk called it. For most of the trip I had my eyes closed listening to sounds or my fingers in my ears looking at the endless beauty all around me.

It was like I was seeing it all for the first time. The air was cold and crisp and there were patches of frost in the shaded places of the narrow dirt road. There were deep ruts and big holes causing the wagon to bounce around and I in turn weaved and swayed and tried to stay in the wagon by any means I could. Mr. Tipps made a continuous clucking sound to the mules and every now and then he would give the reins a slap against the mule's flanks causing them to go faster and me to bounce higher in the spring seat of the wagon.

It was late afternoon when the wagon pulled into the backyard of the home I had dreamed of so much for the last few months. How small the house looked now. Something was different but I didn't know what it was.

My brothers and mother ran out to meet us. They were just the same as I remembered. We laughed and cried as we danced around in the yard. Mommy and the boys were busy carrying my treasures into the house. I ran to the house looking for Daddy but I could tell even before I stepped into the big room that he was sick again. I could hear his heavy breathing and smell the poultices that went with sickness he had.

He was sitting on a short stool close to the fireplace, with a quilt wrapped around him. He was shaking and kind of hugging himself, staring into the fire. He could hardly talk but he managed to say, "Welcome home curly headed baby." He cried. The last time I had seen him at the hospital he was crying and I wondered if he had been crying all this time. Somehow I knew things would never be the same as before. I felt like an old person and I held on to him and hugged him for a long time. I can still feel the texture of his hair and smell the camphor that was in the home remedies Mommy used to doctor him with.

The boys were busy going through the boxes of toys and clothes Miss Linda had sent back. They were laughing and yelling. There were toys all over the floor and the boys were excited because they had never seen so many toys before. I just stayed there with Daddy. He seemed like a child too. He seemed younger than me.

Mommy hadn't said a word. Mr. Tipps came into the room and asked about Daddy. Mommy said, "He's bout the same. I'll shore be glad when summer comes cause the warm weather makes him better. The sun is like medicine to him." She went over to the big willow basket where she kept her yarn and took out a pair of heavy knitted gloves and gave them to Mr. Tipps. She then took her own hat and gloves off and handed them to him also. She said, "They're fer you and Marthy. They're all the pay I can give you."

Mr. Tipps said, "Charity, I don't want no pay. I was glad to bring the girl from town. Never had to go outa my way a bit. I had to pick up some medicine fer Marthy at Doc's place."

Mommy was a proud woman and would do without before she would take something without paying for it. I watched her face, some how she had changed. She stepped over the rubble of toys and little boys and looked up at Mr. Tipps. He was a tall man and Mommy was short but her presence filled the room as she said, "If you don't take them you'll take my pride and that's 'bout all I got left." He took the gloves and hat as he said, "Go with me." That's what everyone said when they left. I've always wondered what would really happen if we had just got up and went with him. I'll bet he would never have asked anyone else to go with him.

Mommy said, "Can't, you all come and see us." He left. I tried to see what had changed and I thought if I took my fancy clothes off and put on my old clothes everything would be the same as before I went away. It didn't work. The clothes didn't change a thing.

Mommy looked so tired. She never stopped working. She put wood on the fire and filled the kettle with water. I knew I must help because I felt all this change was my fault.

Before Mommy went to the barn to milk and feed the animals she told me to look after the two younger boys and for Johnie to bring in wood for the fire. My youngest brother, Toots was small for his age. He was a little over two years old and was no bigger than a six-month-old baby. I was almost seven and could carry him around easily. I wasn't sure what to do for him so I washed his face and combed his hair.

Daddy had laid down on the bed and the sound of his breathing, smell of camphor, and the wood burning in the fireplace filled the room.

By this time the boys had sorted out the toys suited to them and discarded the dolls, little dishes and toys girls usually play with. I picked them up and put them in boxes and pushed them way back under the bed as far as I could reach, out of sight. I felt like the rejected toys.

The baby began to cough and breathe heavy like Daddy. He had the same sickness as Daddy. I held him and tried to comfort him and after awhile he stopped coughing and began to play with the toys again. I was scared because I thought both Daddy and Toots were sure to die.

There was a closet in the corner under the stairway that went up into the loft. We kept the loft shut in the winter because the room was hard to heat. We kept the kitchen stuff in the closet. The pots and pans we hung on the wall around the fireplace.

It was dark when Mommy came back from the barn. She was carrying a basket of eggs and a bucket full of warm milk. It had been so long since I had drunk warm milk and I danced around the room with the baby on my hip waiting for the milk and mush I knew we were going to have for supper.

Mommy was smiling for the first time since I had arrived and she said, "I'm shore glad you're home cause you'll be a big help to me."

I'd seen Mommy's hands before but I had never looked at them really good. Had they always been so red and rough? I looked at my own soft white hands and felt ashamed of them and tried to keep them hidden. Johnie had put wood on the fire and the room was warm as toast. The only light was from the blazing fire and it was all we needed.

Daddy was sleeping and his breathing was easier. I held the baby close and kissed his fingers. He was much smaller than Pretty Baby and his skin was so white. He could say a lot of words. When I left he wasn't talking but now he said everything I said.

After supper I put one of my long Lexington gowns on Toots and slept with the boys and held the baby all night. Somehow I just couldn't find that carefree little girl no matter how hard I tried.

Life went on at the log house. Mommy was up early doing the milking and now that I was home to look after the baby, Johnie went to help with the milking and feeding. Daddy got a little better and now and then he would hum a little tune.

I remember it was my birthday and I woke up to the smell of salt pork and fried mush. It wasn't light yet and I rose up in bed and there was Daddy fixing breakfast. He was dressed and Mommy rose up in bed too. He turned around and said, "Lay low sweet Charity, I'm a Goin' to feed you this morning." I was smiling all over and Mommy was smiling too. It was the beginning of another good day.

The man named Joe came that day to get Mommy to deliver a baby. Mommy was a granny woman and people came from all around to get her to deliver their babies. Some of them paid money, but most of them gave her chickens, meat, a sack of flour or whatever they had to pay. Some didn't have anything to give, but that didn't matter to Mommy. She helped anyone who needed her.

This time when she got home she had a bag of white flour and some money. It seemed like a celebration because Mommy baked cookies on the open fire. While she was gone Daddy cooked shuck beans in the iron kettle and put potatoes in the fire to bake and the room was warm and smelled of good things to eat.

Daddy was a lot better and it almost felt like nothing had ever happened that there had never been an accident and I had never been away from home at all.

The baby that was born that day, on my birthday, was a little girl. Mommy told Daddy it wouldn't live until warm weather. I felt sad and thought about Pretty Baby and Miss Linda. I wasn't asked about Lexington and I didn't talk about it. It was strange that when I was in Lexington I was dreaming of home, and now at home I was dreaming about Lexington.

Mommy always went to check on a new baby and the mother to make sure everything was all right. I begged her to let me go with her to see the new baby. She said if Daddy was still better and able to look after Toots and Bill I could go. Daddy looked at me and winked, he began to sing, "Whoopee Liza, pretty little gal, whoopee Liza Jane."

The next day Daddy was still better and to prove it, he picked the banjo and sang a few tunes. It made us laugh, even Mommy smiled and said we were tricking her but she let me go. She said, "Put on your city clothes but if anyone asks where you got them fancy things, you just say they're Christmas presents, and that will be enough said."

I knew why she felt that way. She didn't pay for them and it went against her grain to take anything without paying for it. I was ashamed of the beautiful clothes Miss Linda had so carefully chosen for me and I wondered if she ever thought of me. Mommy and I walked to see the new baby. It was a long way and after we got off our road, the path was narrow and only one person could walk. It wound around the side of a steep hill. After we got around the hill the path was wider but still a wagon or sled couldn't have gone through. We had to cross a creek and the water looked deep and ice was frozen around the edges of the creek bank. There was a foot log and I was scared to cross it. Sometimes two logs were laid side by side and were much easier to walk but this was just one. Mommy walked across like a dancer. It seemed as if she hardly touched the log at all. I was terrified and could hardly move. Mommy looked at me very hard and seemed mad at me for being such a baby. She said, "Take your gloves off and hold one in each hand and WALK!" I made it across, but the rest of the day I dreaded crossing the log on the way back. After we were across, the road began to get wider and much smoother. A car could have gone through without any trouble at all. We went around a curve and there was a clearing, a sort of a valley. Mommy said, "This is Gale Holler."

There were half a dozen houses scattered around the valley and you could see cattle and chickens. Dogs were barking but there was no sign of people anywhere. Mommy said, "All the folks here are kin. Some never been outa this holler. None of the women ever been to town, cept Soph and she came here before I was born. Everyone else was born here. They don't take to outsiders. The only reason they come fer me is because their Granny died a few years back and I been bringing their babies ever since."

"Don't you be scared honey; I won't let anything happen to you." She patted her pocket, where I had seen her drop the small gun into before we left the house. "Most these folks are feeble minded, all the youngens are. They marry their own kin; it's getting real bad now. Babies have bad hearts and they're real bad deformed. A lot of em comes dead. The baby is purty, but she'll die soon."

As I listened to Mommy, I thought, I'll never marry my kin. I asked Mommy if they had eyes. She said, "Far as I know they do. Why'd you ask?" I was thinking of Pretty Baby and I said, "I don't know."

The house was made of logs, not near as good as ours, all the people looked dirty and funny. The floor was not wood like ours. It was dirt and packed down until it was shiny.

The baby was a pretty baby but it breathed real hard and fast. The mother's name was Nell and she couldn't talk plain and her eyes looked funny, slanted and she had no eyebrows or lashes. Her hair was thin and you could see her scalp through the thin blond hair. She was glad to see Mommy and reached her arms out to her like a child would. Mommy hugged Nell. Nell must have been hard of hearing because Mommy talked loud to her. She said, "How you feeling Nell?"

Nell said, "My baby won't suck Charity, why won't my baby suck?"

"Your baby has a bad heart Nell, it's goin to die." If Nell understood what Mommy had told her, you couldn't tell by her actions. Mommy fixed some sugar water and rubbed it on the baby's lips. She put the baby to Nell's breast and it began to suck. Nell squealed and laughed, she was overjoyed. I watched and was fascinated.

An old woman came into the room. She looked like all the other old people I had seen. She was clean and her hair was combed. She began to talk to Mommy about the patch over my eye. She knew my grandmother and great-grandmother and she asked about people I had never heard of but Mommy knew them. After they had talked awhile they looked at Nell and the baby. They were both asleep and the old woman said, "It's a goin to die, ain't it?" Mommy nodded her head. The old woman said, "I hope they all die, sometimes I think I'll kill 'em myself."

Mommy said, "Hush Soph, don't say that."

Soph said, "Charity I've got some money here, you take it and sew the buryin' clothes fer the baby. Have your man make the box. I'll send Joe after 'em when the time comes. I'd like fer you to come and bring the girl. Just put the dress in the box." She took the money and stuffed it into Mommy's apron pocket. It looked like a lot.

Mommy said, "Soph that's too much."

Soph said, "I got a lot more Charity and I ain't goin' no whar to spend it." Soph reached out to me and raised the patch off my eye; she looked at me for a long time. She looked at Mommy and said, "She's purty Charity."

We went out the door and back down the valley. I was scared and Mommy held my hand. She was scared too. She said, "Get on the other side of me." She put her hand into her coat pocket where I had seen her slip the small gun, just before we left our house. Mommy said, "Don't look back," but it was too late I had already seen the strange animal looking people coming from behind the house we had just left.

Mommy said, "Don't you worry, they'll follow us a little way but they won't hurt us. They need me to bring their sick youngens into the world and bury em when they die." She laughed like she was trying to keep me from being scared. She said, "They always have meat on the table and money in their pockets. The men are the best hunters anywhere. I guess it's because they're so much like animals themselves. They sell the hides and get lots of money, but they don't know how to spend it. Strangers that wander up here don't leave. Joe is the only one that goes out of this holler; he's the only one that's got any sense, him and Soph. I don't know what's goin' to happen here when Soph dies. She's as old as these hills."

We were down out of the valley and near the creek now and I was in deep thought about all those sick babies. I wanted to get home to Toots. I had forgotten about the foot log and I walked right across behind Mommy without thinking about it at all.

The trip home was much faster and not near so scary. Mommy seemed much happier and every now and then she patted the pocket where Soph had stuffed the money.

When we got out of the mountains and on the main road we were both excited and ran a little, like we couldn't wait to get back to normal acting people. We would stop running and look at each other and laugh, and then we would run again. Once when we stopped Mommy said, "I wish I could see a rabbit. I could shoot it and we would have rabbit and dumplings for supper."

I wanted to tell Mommy how pretty I thought she was. She was little with short black hair and big brown eyes that always looked sad even when she was smiling. I didn't know what to say so I held onto her rough red hand and laid my face against it. I just said, "I love you more than anybody." Somehow it didn't seem enough.

When we got home Daddy had a rabbit on the fire already cooked. We laughed as Mommy told him how we looked for a rabbit on the way home. I went to the baby and cuddled him and told him how smart he was. Mommy made dumplings.

Daddy said, "Make a bunch Charity, we'll have rabbit and dumplings and blackberries and dumplings." While we kids played Daddy and Mommy talked about all the way you could fix dumplings. It had been a good day.

Mommy wrote a letter to the storekeeper in town that very night. She put some of the money Soph had given her into the envelope. It was for the material to make the burying dress and the lining for the box. She seemed in a hurry to get started on it. The next day she met the mailman and talked to him. He rode a mule and there were two sets of saddlebags hanging across the mule's back. Sometimes he would have two sacks tied together on the mule also. The bags that had a padlock on them were the mail and the other held things for the people on the route. He would pick up medicine and all manner of things for anyone who asked him. He carried a list, and I can see him as he added Mommy's request to the already long list. He used a stubby brown pencil and after each word he wrote he touched the pencil to his tongue and added the things to the many others on the piece of brown sack paper.

Daddy wasn't going outside yet, but he did a lot of things in the house and he began to work on the box for Nell's baby. I kept asking questions about the baby. How could they know it was going to die? Maybe it would live. Mommy said, "Hush up, it was dying when it was born."

We had such a good day; just seeing Daddy work again was reason to celebrate. I remember how excited my brother Bill was. Daddy had whittled a set of tools for Bill. They were his favorite things. If Daddy was pounding, Bill pounded with his little mallet too. It was funny to see how tired Bill was when the day ended.

We began to have a warm day now and then and the Easter flowers began to push up through the ground. They were along the rock walk from the road to the front door. In spring when the yellow flowers had all bloomed, a third of the yard would be covered. By the side of the road where the first rocks were laid for the walk, was a huge burning bush. Just when the yellow flowers had all bloomed and I thought I would burst from the beauty of it, the burning bush would burst forth and for a whole month there was no keeping me away from that red and yellow display. I would take the baby and we would sit on the rock walk in the warm sun and play for hours. I made necklaces and halos. The baby and I would wear them with such pride. Toots looked funny wearing the flower necklaces and halos and pushing the little cars around and making funny car noises.

Mommy had finished the dress for Nell's baby and Daddy got the box ready. Mommy lined the box with soft white cotton and put white satin on top of that. The box was made from pine. Daddy rubbed the box with fat until it was the color of wild honey.

I asked God to let Nell's baby live. I went again and again and lifted the lid to the box so I could look at the tiny white satin dress, spread out in the box.

Joe came for the box before the yellow flowers were gone. He was a tall man. His clothes were made of leather and smelled terrible. His boots were big; they came up to his knees. He had a gun in his belt, and his hair was black with some gray in it. He had a long black beard streaked with gray. I had never seen such blue, blue eyes.

He wouldn't come into the house even though Daddy asked him. Instead he stood outside and hollered. We kids crowded around Daddy and looked out at the strange man. He looked straight at me while he talked. Joe had two coons with their legs tied together, hung over his shoulder. He took the coons from his shoulder and threw them down on the ground. He said, "They're fer Charity. I got'em fresh jest today. Thar's not a hole in their hides. Got 'em straight in the eye."

Coons were special in the mountains, to everyone. Not only was their hide's valuable but also the meat was very good to eat, very similar to pork, and the fat was used to make lights and to rub on leather and wood. Coons were more valuable than money.

Joe hollered at Mommy, "Charity, we're goin' to put 'er down in the mornin', fore lite. Soph's kept 'er sleepin' all this time. Soph says Nell's most like to die if she gives 'er any more tea. We gota get the youngen down quick."

Mommy said, "I'll be there Joe." Joe left with the box on his big shoulder. We all stood in the door and watched until he was out of sight.

Mommy and Daddy began skinning the coons. They stretched the hides over boards. Daddy said he hoped the weather stayed cool, because the hides cured better in cold weather. That night we had coon for supper.

When I woke the next morning, Mommy had already left for Gale Hollow. She was home by dinnertime. She talked to Daddy about the burying. She talked low so we kids couldn't hear but she didn't know how good my hearing was. All I had to do was close my eyes and listen real hard and I could hear the wings of a fly fluttering in the air.

Mommy said, "I think Soph give Nell too much of that tea cause she's still asleep and some of the others looked like they might have had a goodly dose. They were a nodding like they were ready to fall over right there by the grave. I think some of them wasn't there and that's not like them Gale Holler people. They're clannish, more 'an any other family around here. Something is a goin' to happen in that holler. I can feel it in my bones. It's goin' to be bad." She stared into the fire for a long time and shook her head. She said, "Jim, them people is like animals, all except Soph and Joe." She just kept shaking her head.

The weather was still cool but we had some warm days. Daddy had good days and bad days, but none as bad as when I came back from the hospital.

Sometimes Mommy would look down the road in the direction of Gale Hollow. She would shade her eyes with her hand and stare like she could see something or someone coming up the road.

I told Daddy how much I wanted the little baby to live. Daddy said, "What do you mean honey? That little baby is living in heaven with its Heavenly Father. It's living here in your heart. As long as you're here that baby is living. You don't need to wish it back here. That just wouldn't be right. Maybe we can go up into Gale Holler and put some flowers on the baby's grave."

I said, "Oh can we Daddy? Please can we?"

He said, "Sure we can baby, sure we can."

I would lay awake and watch the logs burning in the fireplace and think Miss Linda and Pretty Baby. I thought about all those babies from Gale Hollow, crawling around in Heaven, playing and laughing and I thought what a good place to be. I told Daddy that I wanted to go there as soon as I could.

He said, "Some day you will, when it's you're time. I will too, you'll see."

Toots got real sick and could hardly breathe. Daddy went to town and got Doc Wally. He said Toots had the same sickness Daddy had. There wasn't much he could do. He gave Mommy some medicine for Toots and Daddy. He told her that Toots might outgrow the sickness. He said, "When summer comes keep him outside as much as you can, take his clothes off and let him go bare. The sun is good medicine for his sickness." It's funny how Mommy already knew that. We looked at each other and smiled.

The next day we saw the stooped figure walking up the road. Mommy shaded her eyes with her hand, the way she always did when she was looking into the sun. She began to run toward the woman. She said, "My God, it's Soph. Something has happened."

I ran behind her. Soph's clothes were torn and she was streaked with blood from top to bottom. She was crying and shaking. Mommy kept trying to find where she was hurt but Soph pushed Mommy's hands away and with a woeful voice she said, "Forgive me Charity, forgive me," over and over again. Mommy put her arms around Soph and held her while she sobbed.

We went to the house and Mommy found clean clothes for Soph and helped her clean herself up. Soph looked a lot like my own Grandmother, but a lot older. Even stooped over she was taller than Mommy.

Soph began to talk, "I could have brought them babies same as you Charity. I jest wanted someone to talk to, someone who had sense enough to answer me. Joe and me had to guard the little girls from them animals. They would have took 'em soon as they walked if Joe and Me hadn't guarded 'em. I've been cooking fer 'em all since we buried the baby. I been putting sleep weed in the victuals. Some died from too much of the weed, and the rest, I killed while they slept, Joe found him a woman over in Laural and he's been spending more and more time there. I slipped in and killed what hadn't died already with a knife. I got scared they wouldn't all be dead so I killed 'em again. Charity, Oh Charity, I'm so tired."

Mommy finally got her to lie down, but she wouldn't lie on the bed. Mommy fixed a pallet on the floor by the fireplace and Soph slept there all night. The next day we looked in the direction of Gale Hollow where a thick black cloud of smoke was rising slowly into the sky. Soph sat outside on a rock by the road and watched the smoke all day. She had a happy look on her face and she told Mommy, "Joe always keeps his word." The next day when we got up, Soph was gone.

Chapter 4

Worst Times

I never knew why the decision was made to leave that place I loved it so much but I think it had something to do with the night we heard the drunken men coming down the road on horses. There had been a killing and families had been fighting. Mommy's brothers had been mixed up in it someway. They had all moved away to Indiana but Mommy wouldn't go.

They had some chickens because you could hear the chickens squawking and the horses were jumping around in the road and the men were cussing. We were all scared, even Mommy and Daddy. We took some covers and ran up into the hollow above the house. We listened and didn't hear anything so we went onto the house. They had been there all right, everything was messed up. They had killed the chickens and pulled the feathers off right there in the house. They had cooked them over the fireplace. Mommy wrote a letter to my Grandmother that very day. About a week later my uncles came in a big truck. Mr. Tipps came with his wagon and hauled our stuff to the truck. Mommy had sold our animals to a neighbor so we had a little money to get started in a new place. We rode in the back of the truck with our belongings.

There was no place to rent and our stuff was stored in a shed at my uncle's house. None of our relatives had enough room for us all to stay together, so some stayed one place some another.

Mommy and Daddy quarreled with each other. Mommy fought with my aunt. There was no work here at all. You couldn't gather nuts and pick berries or wild greens. There weren't any squirrels or rabbits. There was no wood to build things, and no one to buy them. Doctors delivered babies and there was nothing for a midwife to do. We were like animals out of the woods. Everything went wrong.

Daddy had a sister who lived in Indiana, so he took the boys and went to stay with her and Mommy took me and bought a train ticket and we went back to the mountains.

We went back to the house where we had lived but someone else was living there. Mommy found another house. It had two rooms and it sat right by the road. You could step out of the door and into the road. I stayed by myself most of the time while Mommy hoed corn, worked in tobacco or delivered babies.

I missed my brothers and Daddy very much. I cried a lot. I didn't try to hide like I did when we first came back. I'd just sit there and cry right out loud in front of Mommy. She didn't try to comfort me but went on about her work like nothing was wrong at all. I asked her one day, "Let's go get Daddy and the boys."

She said, "They'll come to us, you'll see." I remember being alone one day while Mommy had gone to deliver a baby and I heard horses coming down the road and people were talking and laughing. I kept remembering the time we ran up into the hollow to hide from the drunken men. I was so scared I went into the kitchen and crawled into the cupboard where Mommy kept the kitchen stuff.

I cried so hard then and I prayed for God to take me home with him. I promised him all kinds of things if he would just take me. After the people had gone by I crawled out of the cupboard and ran up into the hills. I found a place to hide. It was a small cave in the side of the hill not far from the house. From then on when Mommy left, I went to my cave in the hillside. I could walk around inside it. I gathered rocks and made places to sit. I picked leaves, wild flowers and gathered moss and made a soft place to lie down. I talked out loud to God and told him how I was going to have a nice safe place for my babies some day. I pretended I had my nice Lexington things there with me, and I pretended Daddy and my brothers were there also.

Time went by and it was time to go to school when someone came to the door. He didn't come in but stood at the door and talked. He said, "Charity, Jim's over to his brother's house. He says to tell you he's got the boys with him and he's not able to come to you." Mommy thanked him and began to get ready to go. It was dark and cool outside. In the mountains the fog hangs in the valleys early in the evenings and doesn't lift until late morning. Nights are always damp and cool. That didn't stop Mommy. I guess she was the strongest, toughest person I ever knew.

We walked the long way to where Daddy and the boys were. I don't ever remember being as tired, as I was that night. I was anxious to see my family and I didn't complain, not even when I stumbled and fell or when I got behind.

I didn't talk to Mommy much after we left Daddy and the boys. I didn't know what to say. I wanted to tell her how glad I was that Daddy and the boys had finally come back, just like she always knew they would. I told her I had been talking to God and he wanted us to all stay together forever and ever. Mommy said, "God told you that?"

I said, "He didn't tell me, he told it to my heart."

She replied, "It would be good if that would happen." I reached for her hand and felt the rough calloused hand close around mine.

It had just begun to get light when we got to the house where Daddy's brother lived. The house sat high off the ground and you could walk under the porch. Everyone was asleep but the dogs. They began to bark and I could hear my uncle yelling at them. The winter wood was kept under one end and the dogs stayed under the other end. We ran up the steps as my uncle came to the door holding a lamp high over his head. He yelled over his shoulder as he laughed, "What'd I tell you Jim, it's Charity and the girl."

Daddy and the boys were lying on the floor on a pallet made from old quilts. Mommy and I lay down on the floor with them and when the sun came up and the fog lifted, we were still on the floor of the old tumbled down shack, a family again.

My uncle helped us find a place to live near the mines. Everything around there was close to the mines. There was store nearby and it belonged to the mines. The houses all belonged to the mines. Our house used to be a store that was owned by the mines also. Someone had used it for a chicken house. We all worked hard to get it cleaned up. It was just one big long room with two doors and several windows. I was very proud of those windows. When the sun came up in the morning, it shone through the windows and warmed the whole house.

The back of the house was built into the hillside. You could climb up the hill and step right on top of the house. The dirt was red clay. The boys played there for hours with their little cars. They built roads by the mile. Toots had grown away from me now and resisted my efforts to cuddle him and treat him like a baby. But at nighttime, when he became sleepy he still came to me. We had no animals now, but Mommy milked a neighbor's cow and got enough milk for us. She sewed clothes for the schoolteacher and got to use the machine for her sewing and mending. The teacher gave her all the scraps and Mommy used them to make quilts for us.

To have privacy, Mommy hung quilts in the narrow room for partitions. We children thought that was a great invention. There was no fireplace but there was a big stove, which we used to heat the house as well as to cook on.

Daddy had gone to work in the mines. He came home for dinner and sometimes some of the other miners came with him. They would pay Mommy for fixing their dinner. Each day when Daddy came home for dinner and at night when the day was over, he would bring a sack of coal with him. Soon the other men did the same thing and Daddy said we had more coal than the mines.

Mommy sure knew how to get by. I think she knew the secret of the loaves and the fishes. I remember it had begun to get cold, but it hadn't snowed yet. We had given the big stove a good test and it passed. Some of the warmer days, we would take buckets up to the sharp curve on the road and pick up coal that fell from the trucks and wagons.

If Mommy wasn't washing or sewing for someone she was making chairs or baskets. There were times when I didn't see her eat for days. I'm sure she did but it must have been when the rest of the family was asleep. When I went to sleep at night she would be sewing, knitting, quilting or making a basket or a chair. When I woke she would be dressed and still working. I sometimes thought she wasn't real, and that she was from some far away place and would just disappear right before my eyes.

She knew what had to be done and did it without complaining, whining or asking for advice, not even from Daddy. I think she knew he wouldn't be around long to turn to, so she didn't get into the habit of depending on him.

All of our things were in Indiana in my uncle's shed. I wonder how many times in my mother's life that she just took her children and walked away, leaving everything else behind. I think she got some strange kind of pleasure out of starting from scratch. I often thought of her as not being human, but some special kind of being who never needed sleep, rest, food, or any of the other things people strive so hard for.

Daddy left for work one morning, but before we left for school he was back at the house. One step and then stop to breathe the wheezy way he did when he was having a bad spell and other step and stop until he was inside.

Mommy helped him to the bed and he sat down. She knelt down and took his shoes off. I remember she almost yelled at us, "You kids get to school." She never raised her head from his feet as she said, "Jim do you want to lay down?"

The last words I heard Daddy say was, "No Charity, if I do I'll never get up again." I saw tears falling on Daddy's feet and Mommy was rubbing them away into the white, white skin of his feet.

I stood outside the door and pressed my face against it and cried. Mommy yelled out again, "are you still there? Get to school." I ran as hard as I could, the tears and snot meeting on my chin, running harder than I was.

We went to school. There was one big room and one teacher. She started the day with the pledge to the flag and a prayer. She stood there in one of the pretty dresses Mommy had made for her and repeated that same unfeeling prayer that she said every day. As she said, "children be seated," At that moment, Bill ran into the room. He was crying and he said, "Daddy has gone to sleep and Mommy can't wake him up." Johnie and I got up and the room full of children quietly watched us leave.

Johnie and Bill ran but I didn't want to go back and I stood in the road in front of the school and I thought, I wonder how long it would take me to walk to Lexington. I began to walk in the direction I thought was Lexington. The teacher stood in the doorway of the school and hollered at me, "honey that's the wrong way."

I wanted to kill her then, I don't know why. I guess it was because she was alive and my kind gentle Daddy was dead. I looked at the teacher for a while, then I turned around and walked slowly back to the house. When I got there the men who ate dinner with us everyday were there. I walked into the room; I don't think anyone noticed me. I went over to the end of the long room. The quilts we used to partition off the rooms were pulled back.

Daddy was stretched on the bed very straight, with his hands folded on his chest. His eyes and mouth were closed. His hair had been combed and his feet were bare. You could hear the quiet in the room. Mommy was standing there beside him with the baby on her hip and a comb in her hand.

I looked a long time. I don't remember what anyone else said or did. I went out into the yard and sat down at the table we kept outside for Daddy and the miners to wash up. There was a bucket of water, a wash pan, and some lye soap setting on it. There were some feed sack towels hanging from nails on the side of the house.

Right out loud I talked to God. I asked him what we were supposed to do now. I told him what a rotten thing he had done. And that he must hate me something terrible, because all I had ever wanted was to be with my family. Now the only way we could be together was if he took us all. I cried and begged him to please take us all. I thought of Soph and I thought I knew how she felt. I looked up and screamed toward Heaven, trying to make him hear me. I got no answer, not even to my heart.

The men brought a wagon and they wrapped Daddy in quilts and put him in the wagon. They took him to his sister's house because they had lots of room for the wake the mountain people always held for the dead. They put him in the parlor and closed the door. Someone built a box and covered it with heavy gray material. It was lined with the same white satin like Nell's baby's box, Daddy had made. The men carried it in and sat it on the floor and went back to get the lid. I looked at it and felt of it. It was soft inside and had its own little pillow.

The men took the box with the lid into the parlor and shut the door. They stayed for a long time. I sat outside and listened to their low muffled voices. I didn't want to hear what they were saying.

People came and brought food and someone stayed awake all the time. The music makers came and sang songs. They came and stood by the box for a long time and said how natural he looked. I wouldn't look at him. His relatives kept trying to make me look at him but I never went into the room to look at the hard stiff body. I knew where Daddy was and it wasn't in that gray box.

I listened to the old women talking. One of them said, "Jim would be alive today if he hadn't run so hard that day with the girl. She owes her sight to him alright." I wondered if it had been my fault that Daddy died.

Daddy was carried to the graveyard in a wagon. The graveyard was on top of a hill and the road wound around the hill. It looked like a giant molehill. When the funeral was over Carter and Betsy took us back to the house. They were Mommy's friends.

Mommy got a coffee sack and went around picking up some things and stuffing them into the sack. She asked Carter to take us to the train. That day, once again, Mommy walked away from everything. We stood there, Mommy, my three brothers and me waiting for the train that would take us to a new beginning.

The train pulled up. Mommy picked up the coffee sack and turned to Carter and Betsy, she said, "You can have whatever is at the house. There are some victuals and clothes, and a few pieces of plunder. Maybe you can get some use out of it."

With nothing but her children and a coffee sack with some clothes in it, she climbed onto the train. She was smiling and humming, "Swing Low Sweet Chariot, Coming For to Carry Me Home."

Chapter 5

The Train Ride

The train station looked like a gathering place for the homeless. Men with coffee sacks and old warn suitcases with rawhide straps tied around them. Women with carpetbags and baskets and some of them had babies in their arms. They stood on the platform waiting for the conductor to yell, "All aboard," before getting on the train. Mommy had been on a train lots of times and she didn't wait for the conductor, she just got right on the empty train and picked out the place where she wanted to sit, right next to the toilet because I got sick when I rode anything with a motor.

She chooses two seats facing each other. The two older boys along with the coffee sack took up one of the seats and Mommy the baby and I sat on the other.

Mommy kept looking out of the window like she expected someone to tell us goodbye or join us on the train, and she just kept humming that tune over and over again.

She let the window down and we watched the people outside. Kids darted around on the platform playing tag. Men in worn, patched overalls with coal dust permanently embedded in their skin, and sad eyed, tired looking women with bellies too big for their coats to button around stood there talking in low tones.

Vendors wandered through the crowd with baskets of fruit, nuts and sandwiches. One man carried pop in wooded carriers, which were suspended from leather straps across his shoulders. There were two little boys dressed alike in black gum boots with their walnut dyed, wool breeches tucked down into the boots. They had sheep skin jackets on and they followed the man around yelling, "Get your pop here." When someone bought a bottle one of them would take the money and the other would hand the pop to them.

The air was heavy with the smell of oily coal smoke, and when the engines got faster the train vibrated in accompaniment. You could hear the conductor yelling, "All aboard for London, Richmond, Lexington, and points north," and the people began to fill the car. The window was still open and Mommy bought some apples from the fruit vendor. She kept looking out the window and the train began to move. Someone was running along beside the train, his white head was barely visible, bobbing up and down with each step he took. It must have been the man Mommy was looking for because she stuck her head out the window and talked to him. The train went faster and faster and Mommy sat back and closed her eyes. We were on our way to Grandma's house and I didn't feel good. I just felt sick. The weaving back and forth and the oily smell of the coal smoke made me sick and I tried to sleep but when I shut my eyes I kept seeing Daddy's face.

We didn't have to change trains at London, but when we got to Richmond we did change and had to wait for what seemed like forever. The boys and Mommy got something to eat at the snack bar in the train station, but I was sick at my stomach from the smoke and the constant swaying motion I stretched out on the bench and pulled my hat down over my eyes to keep the light out and went to sleep. When the train finally came Mommy woke me up. Everyone was looking at us. I guess we really looked strange to them, but they looked strange to me also.

Mommy made all of our clothes and she was a good hand to sew. She sewed for a lot of people and they paid her and a lot of them gave her the left over scraps. She used them for quilts and sometimes they were big enough to make a blouse for me or shirts for the boys. I dropped my gloves and when I picked them up there was a twenty dollar bill right there on the floor. I was so excited. Mommy took it and looked at it like she had never seen a twenty-dollar bill before. She turned all around two or three times and looked at everyone close by. Just then they called for us to board the train to Lexington. Mommy stuck the money in her handbag and got on the train. She later said it really came in handy and that whoever dropped it did us a big favor. If she knew who it was she would have wrote them a letter to thank them, but since she couldn't do that she would thank God. She did too, right there on the train.

The two younger boys, Bill and Toots were all full and tired so they just went right to sleep, but Johnie and I didn't. I was still feeling sick but didn't throw up and was so very hungry. I pulled my hat down over my eyes and just sat there. Johnie was a pretty curious little fellow and he talked to the conductor, who let him walk through the train with him, after Mommy asked him to. She told Johnie to not ask him too many questions and she smiled so pretty at the conductor. I had lifted my hat off my good eye and was watching pretty close to what was going on.

After a long time Johnie and the conductor came back. Johnie had a brown bag of crackers and an apple for each of us. Back then crackers came in a big metal can lined with paper. It looked like a big garbage can and the crackers were big, about five inches square and I was so hungry. I guess Johnie had told him about me being sick and not able to eat, because the conductor told Mommy, "The crackers will settle the girls stomach and the apple would giver her a little moisture." He said, "She needs a little something wet but not too wet." Boy I ate those crackers. Mommy wanted to pay him but he wouldn't take anything but told her he felt like he should pay her because he enjoyed Johnie's company so much. He said, "If you need anything at all just let me know." He walked away and he was whistling. After I had eaten my fill of the crackers I went to sleep and it felt so good to not be sick. I just pulled my knitted hat over my eyes and went off to sleep.

When I woke up we had stopped and everyone was getting off the train. We were in Lexington. Mom asked the nice conductor if we had to change trains. He said, "No but you'll have quite a wait." He said they were changing engines because something was wrong with that one and had to wait for another to come in from Louisville. Mom was always good about finding out things.

She would just smile so pretty and her teeth showed. I thought they were so pretty. When she was a little girl about 8 or 9 years old she got her teeth knocked out at a ball game when someone slung a bat and it hit her in the mouth. It knocked out her two front teeth. They didn't have enough money to have them put in at that time so in the years of her growing up she received a lot of remarks about being snaggled tooth. Her older brothers whipped a lot of kids for making fun of her. She even got married without the teeth. But as soon as she was married she took the cow her mother gave her and traded it for two gold teeth. They were so pretty and she just smiled all the time. But boy her mother wasn't very happy about the trade and never got over her taking a good cow and putting the whole thing in her mouth.

I could hardly believe we were in Lexington. When I was here with Miss Linda we never came to the train station. It was close to Christmas again. It had been a whole year since I had been here and so many things had happened. We all went into the station and it was so big with a ceiling so tall. You could feel the draft from people coming in and going out. Mommy was trying to find a place for us to sit where a draft wouldn't hit us. Toots always had a hard time getting his breath if he got a cold. He was so little and he missed Daddy so much.

The conductor had said it would be a long wait for the train. Mommy had found a place for us to wait so we settled on the long wooden bench. Mommy got two bottles of orange crush in brown bottles and we shared them. It didn't take us long to get rid of that pop.

It was dark but there were lots of lights in the station and people hurrying around and made so much noise. I was wondering which way the hospital was. I sat there for a while with my hat down over my eyes. The boys were still asleep and Mommy wasn't saying anything. I had worn a patch over my eyes since the eye surgery. I was supposed to change it from one eye to the other each day. It looked like a pirate eye patch. I liked to wear my hat. Mommy knitted it and gloves to match. The gloves were mittens. No Fingers in them. They were pretty. She liked me to look pretty. People stared at me because of the eye patch and I would pull the hat down over my eyes, and then just lift it off of my good eye. I thought that was funny. It made me laugh anyway. The doctors said I had to keep one eye covered for about a year and switch the patch so the sick eye wouldn't get lazy, so that's what I did.

Mommy was asleep and I decided I would just step outside the station and look to see if I could tell which way the hospital was. I looked out the big tall wide door and there was nothing there but trains and tracks so I ruled that out. Outside the smaller door was just a plain street and sidewalk. There were stores on both side of the street but none were open. It was very late. There were some lights in the windows and street lights were on. I just didn't remember ever seeing any of that but I figured if I walked out a little ways maybe I would see something I recognized. There weren't any cars on that street at all but up further I could see a few cars going straight through and there were more lights. I walked a little way up the street and stopped then just a little further and stopped again. I wouldn't be able to see down that street unless I walked up there and looked so I just kept going until I reached the stop light and I just stood there for awhile looking both ways trying to see something I recognized, but not a store or anything looked familiar. It couldn't be this close to the train station because I don't remember hearing any trains at the hospital and at Miss Linda's house either. So I decided to go further and straight but I would have to hurry. So I began a kind of slow trot. I didn't see very many people; I guess it was because it was so late. Every time I came to where there was a cross street I looked up and down and after several cross streets there wasn't hardly any houses and no stores at all, so boy I began to get scared.

I turned around and began to run and this time it wasn't a trot it was a full speed run. The next street I came to someone just came around the corner and picked me straight up. My heart was beating so hard I thought it would jump out of my mouth. It was a taller than life policeman. He just held me up and out away from him looking hard at me. He carried me over to the streetlight and said, "I know you. You're Charity's girl. What are you doing here?" I didn't know him at first but those blue, blue eyes I sure had seen before. It was Joe. He had shaved his beard off and cut his hair. He didn't smell bad at all like he used to. He was kind of pretty. I wasn't scared at all. I told him I was looking for the hospital, and I guess I got lost. "Where's your mom youngen?". "She's at the train station," I said. It felt good to be so protected, riding way up high in Joe's big strong arms. I took full advantage of that short trip back to the train station Joe walked back to the station holding me close in his arms and I pretended it was Daddy. I'll never forget that ride. It was just like Daddy was back. In my mind I felt Daddy had just came back for a few minutes to hold me and tell me everything was going to be alright. Joe kept patting me on the back and telling me, "It's going to be alright honey," over and over again.

Joe was one tall man with big broad shoulders and when he stepped into that train station everyone in the station gathered around him. When Mommy had woke up and seen I was gone she had a fit. They were getting ready to start hunting for me.

Joe and Mommy sat down on the bench and began to talk about Daddy dying and Soph and they both cried and he held me on his lap all the time. I was so still and he told her all about how he got to Lexington and got to be a policeman. He had a wife now and was happy. Finally the train engine came and Joe helped Mommy and us kids on the train. He hugged us all and told Mommy to hold on to me. "You'll lose her for good one of these days," he said and walked away never looking back. I just knew I was going to catch it good but Mommy never mentioned it again and I didn't either.

We were all pretty quiet the rest of the way to Louisville. We stopped at Frankfort but didn't have to change trains. When we got off the train at Louisville, Mommy's brother, Ad, was waiting for us. He had been a lot of places and he knew how to get around. He was standing right there at the train when we got off. He always had a funny little smile. It just seemed to always be there. He loaded us in his car and took us to Salem to Granny Catty's house.

I was feeling sick again and Mommy had saved a couple of the giant crackers for me. I swear I think we had a bushel of apples after that train ride. We must have looked real pitiful because everyone that had an apple gave it to us. Mommy just looked and smiled that pretty smile that showed her teeth and thanked them.

I think Joe must have given Mommy some money because she ended that trip with a whole lot more than she started with.

Granny Catty's house always seemed like a homeless shelter. When I think back it seemed she always had a house full of people all the time and she just never stopped working. She always raised a big garden and had pigs and cows and cooked big meals. My uncle Bent, her youngest son was still at home then and seemed to collect a lot of friends. Granny Catty had a lot of nieces and nephews and the nephews seemed to visit and stay a while a lot of the time. Her mother lived with her also, everyone called her Old Granny. She was a funny little lady. She talked a lot even when no one was listening. She seemed to like me a lot and wanted me to sit on her lap although I was a lap full for her. She was afraid I would get cold and was always putting a shawl or something around my shoulders. She never called me by my name at all but called me Nellie. She didn't eat a lot and Granny Catty was always trying to feed her something or trying to fix something she thought Old Granny would like.

There were peddlers who drove big school busses that had the seats taken out and shelves put in their place. They were like grocery stores on wheels, and every Tuesday and Thursday they would come by and stop so you could buy anything from them that you could get in a grocery store. If they didn't have it you could tell them and next time they came around they would bring it. Granny Catty would buy oranges, bananas and candy or anything she thought Old Granny would eat from him. Old Granny always shared with me but no one else that I knew of. She had certain things she did each day and Granny Catty told me to go with her, just to see that she was alright.

There wasn't enough room at Granny Catty's for all of us so Mommy and my two younger brothers, Bill and Toots went to our Uncle Ad's house. Johnie and I stayed at Granny Catty's, but Johnie soon went to our other Uncle Hough's house. He had two boys and a girl. The boys were close to his age. I was kind of lost. I didn't talk much and tried to stay out of everyone's way. I really felt like I was just in the way. I practiced being invisible. I would be real quiet and pretended no one could see me. It worked for me.

Everyday Old Granny and I would go to the barn and pick up the cobs and bring them to the house. Then onto the small orchard near by and we picked up sticks. We would break them up and she would carry them in her apron. She would gather up the edges of her apron and hold it in one hand and use it like a sort of basket or pouch to carry things in. We just wandered around the small farm. Sometimes we would get in the woods and even on the gravel road that went past the house. Old Granny didn't like the road much. She said she didn't mind mud or grass but she sure didn't like little rocks. She didn't even mind big rocks but the little ones she didn't like, and sometimes she would take the broom out and sweep the loose gravel out of the road in front of the house. She would laugh about what road workers would say about that. They didn't come around very often, but she always watched for them.

She never stopped talking to me. She told me about visiting with the Indians when she lived down south and about how they made all their own material and medicine and how they taught her to weave a pattern. She would change her thinking real fast and say we better go out and get some plants. She would name the plants and I wish I knew but they were strange sounding names. When I think back the names sounded foreign to me. I didn't talk much at that time because I was thinking about my Daddy and Old Granny tried to comfort me in her way, by telling me stories about her life when she was a little girl. She told me when she would go visit the Indians, someone in her family would come to get her and she would take another way home and be there when they got back. She would take a stick or her finger and draw the route she took, and she would draw the patterns she weaved like that too. My Granny Catty told me when she was young Old Granny was famous for the material she wove. The store keepers would buy her material to sell in their stores but after her little girl Nellie drowned in the big open well she just never was able to do anything after that. She lived mostly in the past and called every little girl Nellie. One day she was talking to me and I had changed the eye patch from one eye to the other. She said, "What are you doing that fer?"

I told her, "cause mommy said too."

"How long you done that?" she asked.

"Bout a year I reckon," I answered.

She just reached over and took the patch off and stuck it in her pocket. That was the end of the eye patch.

Old Granny didn't talk about the now very often but one day just out of the blue she said, "Where's your daddy?"

I said, "He's dead."

She said, "No – No – No- Sir – Eee," and we went on down to the barn for the cobs and out to the orchard for the sticks, her talking all the time and me listening without comment.

After a few weeks Mommy came back with the boys and a tall white headed man with black eyes. He was very handsome. She announced he was my new daddy. Old Granny threw a fit and said, "No Sir – No Sir – Eee. Nellie's daddy is dead, dead, dead." And she took my hand and we went to the barn and we climbed up into the feed trough and we both cried. I cried much harder at gaining a new daddy than I did at losing the old one, and Old Granny, I didn't know why she cried. I guess it was because I did. The white headed man left and in a few days he came back with a man and a big truck. They put what belongings we had left when Daddy and Mommy were separated before and made a place in the back for us kids to ride. Everyone stood outside and watched us leave. Old Granny stood there and I watched her. Her long dress was almost touching the ground. She was holding her apron with one hand. It was gathered up to make a kind of pouch and it was full of cobs. She wore a bandana handkerchief tied around her thin gray hair and a bonnet over that. She had a large wool shawl around her stooped shoulders.

I was crying as I waved goodbye to Old Granny. She waved her free hand and said, "Goodbye Nellie." As we turned out onto the road I saw her drop the apron and the cobs spilled out at her feet. I closed my eyes and listened to her soft sweet voice going around and around inside my head singing, amazing grace how sweet the sound.

Toots, Bill, & Bert

Chapter 6
Hell Fire & Brimstone

Our lives had changed so much, so fast. We were just little kids and in one year's time we had gone from a very poor happy family living in a small two room house to a miserable angry family living in a big house with two big fireplaces and a home comfort cook stove. The first winter at the big house beside the sawmill was hell. As soon as supper was over and the chores were done we headed for bed because that was the only place we could talk, and then only in whispers. If Black Bob, (which was what our stepfather was called) heard us, he would yell so loud the windows shook, "You God damned young'ens shut up and go to sleep!" We soon learned to be very quiet and when Black Bob was around, if we talked at all it would be in whispers.

We had to feed coal and wood to the fire non stop. Somebody had to keep the hearth clean and the ashes swept up, that somebody turned out to be four little kids. The oldest one just turned ten, I was barely eight, one was five about to turn six, and the baby was three and a half. We just couldn't get used to the new place and the people who went with it. The first couple of days we tried to stay hid but that didn't last long. When we got our orders we were scared to death. The baby was my responsibility, but he always had been and a few more things were added. I had to help cook, wash the dishes, sweep the floors and make the beds; along with anything else I was told. The boys had to help do the feeding, get in the coal and wood, and take out the ashes. There were a lot of animals and that took a long time. None of us could do anything right and you would have thought we were the dumbest kids ever born. Mommy didn't talk to us except to tell us how lazy we were and how we were supposed to know better about everything.

The room we slept in was called the little room but it was plenty big. No heat got in there at all. We kids all slept in that room in the same bed so we could talk and keep warm. I knew how to heat the irons and wrap rags around them and warm our beds, so I did that. I didn't ask anyone, I just did it, but I tell you I was scared stiff. We cried every night. It was like yawning, one started and everyone caught it. We missed daddy so much and we knew he wasn't ever coming, but we missed Mommy too and she was right there with us. She stopped reading to us and talking to us except to fuss at us. She was a new wife now and not a mother anymore.

There was someone else there besides our stepfather and we hadn't seen her yet. She was a lot older than me. She was our stepfather's daughter. She had locked herself in the big bedroom right next to the little room. There was a big nice fireplace in her room, and if the door was left open between the two rooms, both rooms would be warm. The boys carried coal to the door and left it set. Sometimes in the night she would get it without anyone seeing her. We could hear her go into the kitchen at night time and get something to eat and we could hear her crying at night too. Our stepfather yelled and cussed a lot and if we got dirty or our shoes got muddy you would think we had committed the unpardonable sin. We had plenty of food but it seemed like we just couldn't eat much even though we were hungry. I think we were getting skinny. I helped with breakfast. I would set the table and put the butter, jelly, and milk on the table. Mommy did the cooking but we didn't talk like we used to. I took care of Toots. He was a pretty little blond boy. I would wash his face and comb his hair. No one sat down at the table until our step dad was seated, then Mommy would pour coffee and set down and the rest of us would take our places. But some how that morning I just couldn't make myself sit and I began to cry really hard and as usual the boys would cry too. They wouldn't set down. When our stepdad yelled and cussed at us, we all ran into the little room and we were having a real pity party. We just could not stop. I was sobbing and I think the boys were too.

Mommy and Robert started yelling at each other and we heard Mommy say, "Ain't you ever going to make your girl come out and be part of this family? These little young'ens ain't going to sit at this table until she sits first." Things started to change real fast after that little blow up. Robert went to her room and yelled for her to open the door. She didn't and he just kicked it down, clean off the hinges. Well, that stopped our crying real fast and she began to cry. They were cussing at each other, using words we had never heard and of course we added them to our collection of bad words for latter use. He drug her into the dinning room and made her sit down, then Mommy got us kids cleaned up a little and we all sat down. The food was still a little warm and we ate a little bit but we didn't talk or look at Robert or his girl. Robert's girl was named Orme. Right after breakfast she went into her room and started putting some clothes in a sack. Robert asked her what she was doing. "I'm leaving this place," she said. "You're not taking anything with you," he said, and she ran out crying but she didn't take anything with her. She sure hated us and she said it real loud. She went to her brother's house that lived a little ways down the road. We were afraid of him also. He yelled and cussed a lot, and treated his family really bad. Mommy told us they were our brothers and sisters now. There were two older girls who were married and lived in another place. I wished they all lived far, far away. I was hoping Orme wouldn't come back and we could have our Mommy back again.

We all began our chores. The fire had gone out in the stove and I couldn't wash dishes without hot water. You just couldn't make suds in cold water using lye soap so I ran after Mommy and hollered, "Mommy, the fire had gone out," and she yelled back, "start it," and she just went on to the barn to milk. I was crying again and really thought about setting myself on fire. I picked up the little twigs from under the pear tree and all the time I was crying. Toots was following me around saying over and over again, "What's matter? Are you hurt sissy?" I guess I hadn't gotten over all the carrying on and fighting of the morning. I looked everywhere for the matches. There just wasn't any anywhere. I remembered when Tommy Red had come to our house when Daddy was still alive and borrowed some fire because their fire had gone out and they didn't have matches. Daddy shoveled some coals into Tommy's bucket of coals. He was running and the smoke was trailing back toward us from the bucket of fire. I went to the fireplace and got a shovel of coals and put them into the stove and then the little twigs on top but they wouldn't burn. So I figured out I needed to take the ashes out. I tried pulling the ash pan out but it was too hot to handle. I needed an empty bucket to dump them into so I went in and dumped all the coal into the fireplace and I tell you that was a fire. It took off real fast. So I took the bucket and used the dishrags to handle the ash pan. Well, I spilt ashes on the floor but the biggest part hit the bucket. I remembered how my grandma built a fire by wadding up paper and piling sticks and cobs onto the paper and setting it on fire so I did that but I had to make a sort of torch out of newspaper and lit it from the fireplace. Toots was caught up in my crazy actions and was right behind me every step I took. My face had collected a good lot of the ashes and I guess I was a total wreck. When I took the torch to light it, I had to run really fast from the front room to the kitchen. By now the fireplace was roaring from all the coal I had piled on it and when I got to the kitchen the paper had burned almost to my hand. I rammed what was left of that torch into the stove and shut the door on it. When I rose up there stood Robert, Mommy and the boys. Robert yelled loud, "What the hell are you doing?" "I'm building a God damn fire!" I yelled back at him. Toots just hung onto my skirt and smiled so sweet. I looked Robert straight in the eye and didn't move an inch. No one said a word and the boys began to take out the ashes and get the coal and wood in. Robert and I stood there staring at each other. I just know I was going to be beat to death and then I would surely go to hell for cussing. Robert said, "Bert, you'll make a good man one of these days."

It had been a long morning and it wasn't over yet. I still had to heat the dishwater, which I had to draw from the well, and then wash the dishes, clean up the kitchen and dining room and the awful mess of ashes I had made. I cleaned the dining room while the water heated. Mommy had to run the milk through the separator and get a churn ready to make butter. We were all so busy but some how I had bonded with my stepfather without knowing how I had done it. I had a different feeling now that he had let me live, like I was just as good as him and his old mean daughter and son. Toots and the older boys liked the way I had stood up to him and mostly the way I cussed. I some how managed to clean up the ashes and kept the fire going in the kitchen. Robert showed me where to find the matches and his secret of building a good quick fire. He also bragged about what a good fire builder I was.

I still had the beds to make and they all had big feather beds on them. I could fluff them up real good but smoothing them out was hard for me because I was so short I couldn't reach the middle. I used the broom handle, but the broom was so dirty from the ashes I took it outside to beat it against the porch and on my way I looked into the mirror. Boy was I dirty. I just stopped and cleaned myself up and combed my hair. Robert and Mommy were working on the door and I'm sure were watching because Robert went into the bedroom and brought a brand new broom for me to use. He said, "Use that on the bed, that's yours," and he went back working on the door.

After the bed making I went back to the floor. I had made such a mess with the coal and ashes I just couldn't clean it all up. Robert went to the shop and made a dust mop out of sheepskin and rubbed oil into it. That was the best thing I had ever seen. It made the floor so slick and shinny.

Toots just followed me around asking questions and being a baby. We all had so much work to do that we just never got done. There was no electricity and we had oil lamps. They had to be cleaned everyday and that was my job too. I used newspaper. The washing was always a big job but Mommy did that. She had to carry water and we washed on the board. She cooked three meals everyday and there was nothing instant in those days. It was dinner time before I had finished my chores but I had kept the fire going in the kitchen stove and the word was that the house had not been that warm in years.

Mommy could fix a big meal in no time at all but I helped. She peeled potatoes and cook them in butter. She opened a can of green beans and we had left over biscuits and Mommy made chocolate pudding and poured over them. We all ate like little starved pigs and we laughed and talked but we still had that girl to think about. Just out of the blue while we were eating, Robert said, "Charity does you sewing machine work?" She said, "Why yes it does. Do you have something you want sewed?" Robert said, "I was thinking we'd go to town Saturday and get some material for you girls to make Sunday dresses. We'll all go." He turned to the boys and said, "Us men will get a few things too." We were so excited. Maybe this place wasn't going to be so bad after all.

Late that evening Orme came walking around the hill on the footpath from her brother's house. I guess he had talked her into coming home. The door was repaired and I had made her bed and swept up the mess from the door repairs. I didn't touch her clothes or any of her stuff, just the bed. The door was open. Johnie had brought in coal and the fire was going. Robert had opened the door to the little room and it was warm. We had gotten used to the cold room and the privacy of the closed doors. We were all jumpy and nervous about Orme coming home. I expected she was kind of jumpy also. The milking and feeding was done and we were getting supper ready. When she walked in you could feel the tension. She went straight to her bedroom. Robert laid down the paper and said, "Orme supper is ready." She said, "You eat it." He got up and walked into her room. She was fumbling with the door and he said, "I fixed the door but the lock is broken so I took the door knob off, and I took the knob off the little room door also. We need to let some heat into that room for the little kids. Now you get in here and eat supper." He came into the kitchen and she was walking in front of him. We had supper ready and on the table. We all sat down and ate, even Orme. Robert talked about what a wild day it had been, and how hard we had worked and he said, "I think Bert has had the hardest day of us all." I actually smiled at him. I knew he was waiting for a remark so I said, "Yes, it's been the hardest day I've had so far but I've sure learned a lot of things." Everyone but Orme laughed. I asked if he was finished with the paper and he said he was and he wanted to know if I wanted the funnies and I said, "I wanted the whole thing." I told him I noticed it was the Lexington Leader and I always wanted to know what was going on in Lexington. No one laughed at me but everyone smiled even Orme. From then on you might say Robert and I were paper partners. If I wasn't there when he finished with the paper he would fold it back the way it originally was folded and no one else

After they agreed on prices and Robert had paid him they shook hands. Then Robert said, "You know my girl Orme, well she needs a job. She's finished the eighth grade and she can figure and read good. She's a big strong healthy girl and knows how to do any kind of work. I want you to try her out and if she don't please you, just tell her and she'll come on home and you won't owe her nothing." He looked at her a little bit and said, "Send her in Monday morning." Everything was working fine. I sure wanted her to go to work. Before we left town Robert went to a little restaurant called, "The Den." It was in a basement and they served spicy foods. He got some chilidogs. That was a new food for all of us and we really loved them. He got pop and something called moon pies. We ate on the way home. It was such a good day except for the new sleeping arrangement I had to face that night.

It was late when we got home but we didn't have to get supper. We just did the regular chores and popped some popcorn. Mommy and Orme got all the catalogs and we picked out dresses we liked and wrote our names on them and Mommy cut out patterns for Orme's dresses out of newspaper that very night so she could have a new dress for Monday. They got a home permanent for Orme and they put it in her hair that night. Robert and I read the paper and the boys worked on some slingshots. All boys had to have slingshots back then. There was laughing and talking and it was really nice. I hadn't had too much time to think about bedtime but when I did it just made me want to cry but I didn't. I put the irons in the boys' bed like always and Orme fixed the fire. Toots started to cry and I had to talk to him a little. Orme told him if he didn't cry she would bring him a surprise from work Monday and he was happy with that. I was the one who cried. I just felt so bad and when I got in bed I laid on the very edge of the bed and Orme told me if I would move over close to her I would be warmer but I told her I was warm enough and just laid there and cried until I fell asleep.

I remember before I fell asleep she kept moving over a little closer to me. Sometime in the night I woke up and I was so warm and Orme was really close to me and I was right on the edge of the bed and when I started to move I fell out of the bed. It scared everyone and they all jumped up and came running into the room. It seemed I could never stay out of trouble. Orme didn't know what to say, I didn't either. I had to quit being such a baby and stop crying so much, and Mommy told me that. Robert started to say something to Orme but when she put her arm around my shoulder and said lets get into bed, no one said anymore and we all went back to bed. Orme reached over and pulled me close to her and we went back to sleep.

None of us went to church on Sunday after the chores. Mommy started working on Orme's dresses. Orme and I got dinner that day so Mommy wouldn't have to stop working. Robert fixed a place for me to hang my clothes, and he moved my trunk into the girls' room. Orme did the hems and all the handwork on her dresses. By Monday Orme wore one of her new dresses to work, and her hair looked so pretty, all curly and fluffy with her new perm.

We had all the chores done and supper ready when Orme got home that night. We kids were so excited about Orme coming home. We were right at the door waiting for her and asked her all kinds of questions. We were annoyed she didn't get dirty at all and we were all talking at once and I think she had tears in her eyes. That night we had no trouble at finding something to talk about. We left the table still talking and laughing. Orme kept her promise about the surprise, there was a sack of candy and all of us shared it. She had opened up the candy monster in Toots.

I think Robert liked me a little, he never said so or touched me but I heard him talking to Mommy and he said, "Why don't you start sewing on Bert's dresses?" She made all kinds of excuses why it could wait.

She said I had all kinds of dresses but Robert told her they weren't new and she had made Orme's right away and Orme had enough dresses. He told her to start on them that day and she did but it took her a lot longer than a day and I think she did that on purpose. She wasn't used to taking orders and she never did get used to it.

Orme taught us all how to play cards and almost every night before we went to bed we sat on a rug in front of the fire in the girls' room and played a game of cards by the light from the fireplace.

Orme never forgot to bring something to Toots from the store, and after she had been there awhile she bought some new pretty dishes and big roll of outing flannel. She asked Mommy to teach her how to make a pattern. She said she was going to make us all a gown and nightshirts for the boys. I tried on my new dresses for Orme so she could see how pretty they were. Before winter was over everyone in the house had a new gown or nightshirt and they were all white with a little blue flowers on them.

It seemed as if the good times never lasted long for us at the big house. Johnie was the oldest and more was expected out of him. Bill was younger than me and wasn't a whole lot of help. Orme was working full time at the store and only was off on Sunday so things just kind of slipped into a state of almost disaster all the time. Robert and Mommy would spend a lot of time going to the hills, marking timber to be cut as soon as it got warm and looking for a place to build a tobacco bed. Then they would work in the shop and on the old sawmill engine. There was a grist mill too and they were getting ready to run that on Saturdays. Belts had to be repaired and coal hauled in from the mines to fuel the big engine. Sometimes Robert hired Tommy Red to work for him at the mill but he tried to make do with Mommy and us kids most of the time.

When Robert and Mommy would go on the trips through the woods we kids would change the rules. I would help the boys do the outside work and they would help me inside. That worked pretty well. Bill was too little to do a lot of things but he was the most willing worker of us all. He loved to chop wood but he was not supposed to. Robert kept the ax really sharp, and we used a lot of wood in the cook stove. We had lots of ends from logs at the mill and Johnie would split wood but sometimes Bill would slip out and split wood like crazy until we caught him, which we always did. Johnie and I were finishing at the barn and Toots came running to meet us. He was crying really hard and trying to tell us something, which we couldn't understand. We meet Bill walking from the mill to the house and his foot was covered with blood. It wasn't a long way from the house but we made a packsaddle with our hands and carried him to the house. We could carry a pretty heavy load like that. When we got his shoe off he had a pretty bad cut so I got some water and soap and washed his foot really good. I poured clean water over it but he didn't want iodine on it so I just put some yellow colored salve on it and wrapped it good. Then I fixed a place on the rug in front of the fireplace and made him lay there. We had to watch for Robert and Mommy because we weren't going to tell them about Bill's foot. We went ahead and finished the housework and Johnie went down and drug a log chain through the blood back and forth on the path until you couldn't see it. We burnt his socks in the fireplace and Johnie washed the ax real good. I cleaned his shoes really good and then I got to thinking we had all better clean our shoes so Mommy would think we just decided to clean our shoes. We like to have never got Toots into the house so we could do his shoes. He had watched Johnie dragging that chain up and down the path to the mill and he liked that so much he just wouldn't stop. He played with that chain for weeks. We told Bill to pretend he was sick and he did a really good job. He lay on the rug in front of the fireplace in the girls' room and we kept the fire going real good and when Robert and Mommy got in late that evening they didn't make Bill go to the barn. We had done a lot of the work that we could do early. I'll never forget how hard Johnie worked and he didn't say too much about it except to us kids. We were really loyal to each other and if we said don't tell anyone then not one of us would breathe a word of it not even Toots.

By this time I could cook a mean kettle of soup. Mommy had taught me about using the leftovers for different things and I had made a big kettle of vegetable soup and a pan of corn bread. Mommy just tasted it and if it needed anything she would add it or tell me what to add. Orme could cook too but usually she didn't get in until we already had supper ready. She would eat and we had become friends and actually liked each other but not enough to share some of that loyalty that we little kids had with each other.

It was still cold enough for irons in the bed and when I put them in the bed Johnie told me he was going to run away. I was hurt so bad over that, I felt like I would never be able to stand up straight again because my heart felt so very heavy. He said not to worry he wasn't leaving until the weather got warmer because he would have to walk and he didn't want to walk in the snow or ice. Bill wanted to unwrap his foot and look at it but I told him about the time Toots cut my thumb almost off with the corn knife and how I just held my thumb on because I was afraid it would fall off, and I made a fist and just held my thumb straight and wouldn't let anyone touch it so Mommy just wrapped up my whole hand and it stayed that way until the Doctor stopped by on his way to visit an old person who lived up past us. When he looked at it he said I had done the right thing because it had already begun to heal. He took off the bandage and poured some stuff on it and told me to hold my thumb on and not let it drop off and he wrapped it up hand and all. It cured up in no time. Bill was okay with that. I told him I would fix it while Mommy was at the barn and that's what I did. It had already begun to look pretty good and in a couple of days he was going to the barn again helping Johnie.

Orme kept asking me what I was thinking about. She knew something was bothering me because my card game was getting bad. It was useless to ask me because I always blamed it on missing Daddy. If he knew how many times I've used his death as an excuse for my actions. I dreaded for warm weather to come but it was here and Robert and Mommy were getting all the tools together to go up on the hill, they called it the flats, to make tobacco beds. Robert had hired Tommy Red to cut some timber up there and they were going to use the limbs and burn a big place to keep the weeds from growing. Mommy would sow some garden seed as well as the tobacco seeds. We all went for that and it was a lot of hard work but it was fun and we would fix a lunch to take with us and I always like that. I loved the hills in Kentucky. You could find the prettiest places without even looking. We were close to a spring and Robert would tell tales about when he was a young man and played poker up in the hills with his buddies and they would build a fire and set there by the spring. Seems he was always able to find a bottle or tobacco can or a tin can he could tell you what year he had left it there. I never knew if he was lying or telling the truth, but at the time I guess I believed him.

I think it was the next day after we sowed the tobacco bed that Robert told Johnie and Bill to take the mules to the creek and let them drink. They had never done that before and I know they were scared of the mules; they were big and kind of wild because they were so young. Mules are funny and stubborn. Bill was so little and scared. I can't believe Mommy let them lead those wild mules but she did. Just about the time they got to the creek the mule raised its head way up high and jerked the lead rein out of Bill's hand and began to run. Bill began to cry and Johnie turned loose of the mule he was leading and went to Bill.

By that time I was out of the house with Toots and it was another one of those disasters. Robert and Mommy had seen it from the barn and they came running, Robert yelling and cussing as loud as he could. Tommy Red was working at the mill that day and he helped round the mules up, but not until Robert had said a lot of bad words, which we were used to by this time, but the thing he said that us kids never forgot was, he couldn't depend on a herd of weak assed kids because we were just like our no good weak assed Daddy. Johnie just turned around and began throwing rocks at Robert and Bill and I started carrying them to Johnie. Johnie was just pelting him with rocks. Mommy tried to get Johnie and make him quit but Bill and Toots almost tore her dress off to keep her away from him, and I just kept carrying rocks. Tommy Red walked over with the mules and handed Robert the reins and said, "Rob, why don't you pick on something your size. I'm going home." Johnie quit but he went in the house and changed his clothes and rolled up a shirt and a pair of overalls and walked away toward town. Johnie was older than me and knew a lot of things I didn't. He went to the poolroom in Manchester where my uncle used to own. I didn't know that until much later but he stayed there with my uncle's brother-in-law and they put him on the bus to Indiana, and called my uncle and he met him at the bus station in Indiana and took him to my grandma's house. What a blessing my grandma was for us little kids.

Of course we kids that were left didn't know that at the time and Mommy and Robert had a terrible argument over the whole thing but it didn't change anything because Bill and I just had that much more to do. So I started sleeping with the boys again. This time no one interfered but Orme and she tried to get us all to come and sleep with her and we would laugh because she knew all too well what we were going through, after all she had been there all her life.

Orme still brought things from the store for us but she would give it to Toots to hand out. None of us ever had any trouble sharing. It just seemed so odd and funny how much we loved each other, and we still do.

The next week Mommy got a letter from Johnie. He was all right and he wanted Mommy to send him some clothes. The next day she put some things into a coffee sack and sewed the top together. She addressed it to Johnie in care of Grandma and sent us kids to the post office with it. It was a treat for us. We loved to go to the post office. The postmistress was such a nice person and her name was Ruthie. She always cooked something for us, usually cookies or cupcakes. We got to walk by the house where we lived and where we loved so much when Daddy was alive. Needless to say we would always cry.

Johnie was the oldest and he was gone so now I was the oldest and that meant that I would be expected to look after the young ones which I did anyhow but now I kind of felt like I was the boss of the two little boys. I had to carry the sack most of the way even if I was the boss. It wasn't really that heavy but I just got tired and Bill tried to carry it and he did for a little ways, but I would have to take it again. We finally got there with the sack of clothes, and I was so glad. Ruthie gave us some cookies like she always did and a glass of milk. She had the prettiest dishes. She asked us a lot of questions but I didn't know the answers to most of them. When we came back we were rested so we could run a little way. When we came back we stopped at the old at the old house where we used to live and we picked all the Easter flowers we could carry. They were growing all over the yard and the side of the roads. It was so beautiful. Since I was the boss I decided we would take them to Daddy's grave, so when we got to the place where you turned off to go home we just kept going to the grave yard where Daddy was buried. It took a good while longer and I knew we were in for it but we were so excited. There wasn't a stone on Daddy's grave but I knew we were in for it but we were so excited. There wasn't a stone on Daddy's grave but I knew pretty well where he was buried and we scattered the flowers all over his grave and we were so happy to be doing that. We just threw the flowers up in the air and let them fall. We laughed and danced on the ground around his grave. When we left we told him goodbye and we waved all down the hill.

When we got to the house it was time to do the chores and Mommy was mad. She blamed me because I was the oldest and began to yell just like Robert did when he was mad. I backed away from her and the boys were behind me. She slapped me in the face hard, one side and then the other. I just stood there. It made me stager a little but I didn't fall down and I didn't cry a tear I just started walking toward her and when she raised her hand to hit me again I put my arms around her waist and held on real tight but I didn't cry. She just set down on the ground with me and held me for a long time. It had been months since she had even hardly touched me.

She got up and got ready to go to the barn to milk and the boys went with her. I began to get supper ready and I heard Bill and Toots telling her about the flowers and that we had visited Daddy and how we had talked to him and danced around his grave. I made potato soup that night and when Orme came home she brought a big bag of crackers and she tasted the soup and helped me season it up and we held on to each other and cried for a little while. That night she begged us to all sleep in her bed and we did.

Chapter 7
She'll be Coming 'Round the Mountain

The big house and sawmill we looked at from the ridge a year earlier while Daddy was still alive was now our home and I could stand in the bottom of white clover and look up at the ridge where the nut trees and the little blue flowers grew so profusely, wishing Daddy was still alive and the scene would reverse.

The distance from the house to the woods where we picked huckleberries and mountain tea seemed miles away when I was a child and on the day when we children had free time we would walk the long distance through the field of thick white clover.

Just inside the woods was a massive oak tree where Daddy and Mommy brought us when he was still alive. It was by far the largest tree in the forest and as far as us children were concerned it was the biggest tree in the whole world. Its large limbs reached out in all directions refusing to allow anything to grow in its sheltered space. There was a spring near by spewing up out of the ground and running down the sloping hill into the creek below.

Huge ferns grew along the stream and dark green moss, damp and soft was everywhere. It never occurred to us kids that someone else considered that place special also. One of those people was our Uncle John. He lived just a few miles away and it was common knowledge that he had a still somewhere in the hills nearby.

When John was nineteen years old he was injured in a coal mine accident and his legs had to be removed just above the knees. He made a very good living making and selling moonshine. He always had more money than most people around and it seemed when times were the worst he always showed up, riding his little short mule with a roll of money for my mother.

Uncle John didn't use a saddle; instead he rigged up a sort of ladder from ropes which he fastened onto a saddle blanket. The whole business was then fastened onto the mule with a saddle girth. He didn't use wooden legs or crutches but wore padding on his stubs that looked very much like helmets. At that time he was probably thirty years old. He was very strong and muscular in his arms and shoulders. He could reach up and grasp the rope ladder with one hand and swing himself upon the small mule almost effortlessly.

The first week we came to the big house by the sawmill, Uncle John showed up on his little mule. He rode right up to the porch, not bothering to get off the mule and we all went out to see him. He reached into his pocket and pulled out a pint jar full of moonshine and tossed it to my stepfather like it was a ball. Black Bob was a drinking man and he caught it with great care.

"Want ya all t' be happy," he said, and reached into another pocket and pulled out a brown paper bag and handed it to Mommy. "There's some purtys for the young'ens in there and a little something' fer ya too. Can't let ya come to Black Bob without a little nest egg t' help ya hold yer head high. Take care of 'em Bob." And without waiting for comments of thanks, he turned around and rode away the same way he came.

There were pocket knives for my brothers, a roll of money with a rubber band around it for Mommy and a wrist watch for me. I treasured my watch. As far as I knew I was the only one in the whole county who owned a wrist watch. Even the school teacher didn't have one. Hers was on a chain around her neck.

After Johnie ran away to Grandma's my two younger brothers and I spent most of our free time in the woods. We became expert gatherers of mountain tea, dewberries or any edible thing common to that part of the country. Wild greens were our specialty during the spring months. It was known to everyone that polk, speckled doc, dandelions, violets, groundhog, wild mustard and the tiny little sprouts from the berry briers, also the new fronds from the massive ferns and water cress all grew plentiful along the woods by the big oak tree and down along the stream that ran from the spring to the creek.

The spring thaws and rains ran down the spring fed stream washing away the dirt until I could stand upright in some places and be totally concealed. We children played in the water in the warm months and sometimes when it wasn't so warm. Mommy didn't know that we took our clothes off and hung them on the bushes and like wood nymphs we ran up and down the cold stream splashing and talking about the time we would build a house there in the woods and leave Black Bob and Mommy forever.

We tried all kinds of magic tricks and spells, like making miniature images of our stepfather from mud and we would circle round and round the mud dolls, chanting all the curse words we had ever heard and we made up a few of our own. Sometimes we would smash the mud dolls with rocks and other times we would spear them with spears fashioned from the iron weeds that grew around the edge of the woods.

On those trips to the woods we most always rode our stick horses, also made from the iron weeds. We put the gathering buckets (which were four pound lard buckets) on the head end of the stick horses and rode off in great style at a very high rate of speed to the woods and the big oak tree, which was always our goal.

I remember the time I left my watch at the spring near the big oak tree. We had been playing in the water and I hung my watch on a bush beside the spring. It got late and we climbed on our stick horses and rode fast down through the clover field to the big house. I didn't notice the watch was gone until we were getting ready to go to bed. My baby brother always wound the watch, but when I started to hand it to him, it wasn't there. I was scared so bad I though my heart would stop. I knew I had earned a number one whipping and there was no way I was going to get a chance to pick the switch. I couldn't sleep at all and I thought about running away but I decided better. I would wait until everyone went to sleep and I would slip out of the house and go to the woods where we played and get my watch.

The moon was shinning and there was fog hanging in the low places along the creek and branches. The dew was heavy and with the moon so bright the white clover field looked as if a deep snow had fallen during the night. There were deep black paths left by leaping deer the length of the field, right up into the woods. The scent of honeysuckle was strong in the damp night air.

I hadn't put my clothes on because I was afraid I would wake up my brothers. So barefoot and wearing only a night gown I ran the full length of the meadow, following the path made by the deer into the woods, past the big oak tree and down into the ravine to the spring. Sure enough there was my watch hanging on the bush where I had left it. I put it on and almost crying with relief I started to climb out of the ravine when I heard the clop clop of a horse coming from the other direction toward me and the oak tree.

I was so scared I slid back down into the ravine. My heart was pounding so loud I put both hands over it to muffle the sound but it just moved up into my ears and I was sure everyone in the world could hear it beating. I pressed by body hard against the cool mossy bank of the ravine as the sounds of the hooves came closer and closer.

It stopped beneath the oak tree. I held my breath and I got enough courage to peep up over the bank. It was Uncle John. He looks so funny on the little mule with his little short legs sticking straight out. His arms and shoulders were massive. His neck was big like a wrestler's and he was clean shaven. He wore bib overalls and denim jacket with lots of pockets. He always carried things in them to give to the young'ens he happened to meet.

I stayed hid but every now and then I would rise up to see what he was doing. "God please make him leave, please," I prayed. There was no way I could get out without him seeing me. I looked again and I was doomed. He began to take his clothes off. He took off the coat and then unbuttoned the bib of his overalls and let them hand down while he emptied his coat pockets and put everything in his overall pockets. He began to feel around in the leaves, picking up the sticks, pebbles and acorns, tossing them over into the ravine where I was hiding. "My God, he was making a bed. I wish he'd never give me that old wrist watch, and then I wouldn't be here hiding like I'd done a bad thing."

He was fluffing up the leaves and dragging in some fresh ones. He took the little mule around to the other side of the tree and tied it to one of the huge limbs, then came back to the bed waddling like a duck on his stubs, balancing himself with his big muscular arms.

He was singing now, "She'll Be Coming 'Round the Mountain When She Comes," and all the time he was working on the bed. He took his coat and shirt and spread them over the pile of leaves being careful not to get on it or mess it up. He sat down and removed the leather helmets from his stubs and threw them against the tree trunk.

I hadn't ever seen his bare stubs and my eyes were fastened on the spectacle. The overall legs had been cut off and folded over the ends of his short stubs. I was so engrossed in the undressing of Uncle John I didn't see Betty come into the woods until she was right up close to Uncle John. Neither one of them was one bit surprised at seeing the other one there. Uncle John's state of undress didn't bother Betty at all and she began to unbutton her shirt and added it to the pile of leaves. When she took her big gathered feed sack skirt off and threw it on the pile I thought I was going to die. I held my hands over my mouth and put my face into the mossy bank and cried a little.

It didn't take long for my courage to return and I peeped up over the bank again. Betty was bare foot, in fact she was bare all over and so was Uncle John. Betty was a big woman and everyone mentioned her said she was a handsome woman. I wasn't sure she was handsome but one thing for sure, her bare breast looked just like the hog bladders at butcher time. Mommy always cleaned the bladders and blew them up for us to play with. They would last for a long time without bursting. She was on her knees with her bare rump right toward me and it looked like Uncle John's mule's rump except Betty didn't have a tail. With her on her knees and his little short legs, they were the same height. The hugged each other and kissed, flat in the mouth a bunch of times. John took the pins out of her hair and reached over and picked up his overalls and put the pins in his pockets. She liked that a lot because she kissed his face and arms and even his big broad hairy chest. They sure didn't talk much but they hugged each other and rolled around in the leaves and the leaves were sticking to their bodies and in their hair but they were still rolling around like two giant wrestlers trying to pin each other down.

I slid back down into the wet damp moss praying they would go away and thinking how crazy I was slipping out in the night and coming so far into the woods alone. The quiet and cold began to bring me back to the trouble I was in. I should have told Mommy and took my licking and got it over with. I thought what some fools would do to keep from getting a licking.

Once more I peeped up over the edge of the ravine and Betty was on her knees, her long straw colored hair touching the ground while she smoothed out the leaf bed and spread the clothes out over the leaves. Still on her knees she straightened up and slung her head to get the hair out of her face. Some of the leaves fell out and John leaning on one elbow picked the rest of them one at a time from her hair. I guess she was pretty enough, any how her smile was nice and her teeth were white and even.

They lay back on the freshly made bed and talked in low voices that I could not hear and after awhile they got up and began to dress. I guess John felt bad about wrestling with Betty because when he gave her hair pins back he counted out some money to her. Betty left the woods first. She looked back over her shoulder and waved her hand in the air and said, "see you next week Johnny," and ran down through the field of clover.

Uncle John began to whistle, "She'll be Coming 'Round the Mountain When She Comes," and walked straight toward me. I put my hands over my eyes and tried to bury myself in the mossy bank, but John had seen me.

"Young'en what the hell are you doin' here in the woods? Your Ma'll take a strap to ya, and that's a fact." He came sliding down the bank and I was crying hard now.

"How long ya been here? Did ya see me ride up?" I shook my head, yes. He lay down and drank for a long time from the spring and then he stuck he whole head in the spring and got up and shook the water from his head like a wet dog would, then he looked at me for a long time. I was barefoot wearing only a night gown and my wrist watch. "I forgot my watch," I said.

He shook his wet head again and grabbed hold of the oak tree's roots where the water had washed the dirt away leaving them bare and clean like long bony fingers trying to get a hand full of dirt, and he pulled himself up out of the ravine and reached his big arm down and pulled me out of the ravine. He got the mule and like he pulled himself out of the ravine he held onto the rope ladder and swung himself onto the mules' back. He pulled me onto the mule and we rode back down the bottom of clover. The sun had come up and the illusion of snow had disappeared. When we got to the house Mommy and my stepfather were getting ready to search for me.

John helped me off the mule. He didn't get down himself but he looked at Mommy and said, "don't whip 'er Charity. I found 'er at the big oak. Fergot 'er watch an' went to fetch it 'fore ya found out. All of us ferget things now an' again. Take me, now I fergot my pads at th' big oak where I was a restin'."

He waved his big arm, winked at me and slapped the mule on the rump a couple of times and it began to run. The overall legs were hanging down flapping in the breeze and he was singing, "She'll be Comin 'Round the Mountain When She Comes."

Granny Catty

Chapter 8
Thank God for Grandmas

It seemed we no sooner got used to one thing than something happened to change things all around and we had to get used to something else. Now Robert and Mommy started working everyday at the sawmill and Tommy Red and one of the Bowling boys came to help saw logs into lumber. On Saturdays the belts would all be changed and the gristmill would operate. We still had all the other chores to do, and there was that big garden. I began to see why Robert married my mother. She knew how to do almost everything and wasn't afraid to work and I guess he counted us little kids as extra workers also. He didn't know us very well though. We were a lot more independent than he bargained for, after all he had lost the biggest and the best worker with his bad dirty mouth, and when the grown ups weren't around we were constantly planning how we were going to run away also. We would swear to never tell what our plans were.

Johnie wasn't there to help and I had to help with a lot of the outside work. When I did that a lot of the time the only bed I had time to make was the one that was in the front room and I would shut the doors to the other rooms so the kitchen, dining room, and the front room was all I could do and Bill would help me and I would help him. It was getting warm and there were not so many fires to keep going and that helped.

Orme would help after she got home at night and we sure were glad to see her coming up the road. She would ride to work with her brother but she had to walk to his house in the morning and back in the evening. On Saturdays they stayed open late at the store so it was always late, even dark most of the time when she got home. Robert owned a couple of houses that he rented out and there was a widow woman who lived in one of them and he hired her to do our washing sometimes and that was such a big help to my mother.

After the mill started up Mommy had to work at the mill so a lot of the work at the house was left up to me. Bill and Toots would help, but Toots just followed us around and asked silly questions. There was never a day that was work free. In the spring we always washed all the bed covers and carried the bedspreads and mattresses outside to be cleaned and aired, but the quilt washing was the most fun. We had a big huge iron kettle that looked like a mixing bowl and it was placed on some big rocks close to the branch that ran into the creek. The kettle was big enough you could dip a hog in it and scald it, which we did when we killed hogs. We used that kettle to heat our wash water in the warmer months. Mommy would put three tubs down on the ground and put water in each one. The first one had soap in it and us kids would get in and stomp the quilts until they were clean. Then she would move it to the next tub for rinsing and the last tub for a final rinse. The last tub she would ring out the quilt and hang it on the line. We like stomping quilts. Our little feet would be so wrinkled.

There was another job we had to do in the spring and that was clean out the stables in the barn. There were about eight stalls, and Robert would park the sled in front of the stall and we would fill it up and he would scatter it on the fields and park it back for the next day we did that until all the stalls were clean. When we did that we could clean up in the creek before we came in the house.

Saturday was grist mill day and if anyone was at the mill when dinnertime came Robert always invited them to come to the house and eat with us and they always did. I was the cook. Every Saturday we had soup and corn bread. There were just two kinds of soup I could make and that was vegetable and potato soup. I was told it was never the same but the reason was my leftovers were always different. But Mommy would always taste it when she came in and if it needed anything she would let me add more seasoning. Robert would brag about my cooking and tell everyone about how I could build a fire and how warm the house had been since I had been there. Everyone who ate on Saturdays liked my potato soup the best. I had to make a big kettle because the table was full and we kids had to eat after everyone else. I really didn't know why it was liked so well but when I think about it I would say it was the cream and butter I put in it. I would use a whole bunch of pure cream. If we had a lot of butter and usually we did, I put a lot of butter in also.

I could tell Mommy wasn't very happy because she was used to helping people and Robert didn't like for her to deliver a baby or go to someone's house to help with a sick person. She would go if someone came for her, but the word got out because of the way Robert acted when they came to get her. People would come to get her and he didn't like it. When she came home from delivering a baby you could count on a fight. Mommy was more like a slave than a wife I would say and that led to a lot of fights. She was just a little person and if she sat down to eat sometimes she would fall asleep right at the table.

We didn't go to church as much as we used to and the church was real close to our house. All of a sudden Mommy announced that we kids needed to go to church more often. She told Robert right at the table that we were not working on Sundays anymore. She said God would not forgive her for keeping us away from church. It was just so exciting to watch our little puny Mom stand up to Robert. So he said he had read the Bible a bit and he remembered somewhere in there it said if the ox was in the ditch on Sunday you could get it out and Mom came back with "We've been here going on a year and the ox has been in the ditch everyday." There was a long discussion about the Bible and I think Mommy won because on Sunday we went to church. We had a battery radio and on Saturday night we could listen to the country music station. But Mommy sat up real late getting our clothes ready for church. I stayed up and helped and we would listen to the Grand Ole Opry while we worked. It was so good to do that with her. Mommy went to church with us. Robert and Orme stayed home. There were a lot of our friends we didn't get to see often and Mommy talked and laughed and it sure was good to see her do that. She looked so pretty and her teeth showed.

I remember going to church when Daddy was alive. That was our main social event and we always looked forward to it. I always thought God was just setting on the rafters that were in the open ceiling over the pulpit because the preacher would always look up in the ceiling and hold her arms up when she prayed. She told us all to bow our heads and close our eyes but I looked and her head wasn't bowed and her eyes weren't closed and her arms were reaching right up to the ceiling towards God. Well I wanted to see God too so I slipped out of my seat and crawled on the floor under the seats toward the pulpit. I figured I would have to do it while all eyes were closed and all heads were bowed. We always sat up front real close. If she prayed a long time she wouldn't see me. Obviously there were more than the preacher and me who weren't closing their eyes, my mommy was one of them and my whole family, and I think all the kids. Suddenly Mommy reached under the seat and grabbed my foot but I kept crawling and left her holding an empty shoe. I had a date with God and no one was going to keep me from seeing him. The boys were giggling and so were all the little kids and a few of the grown ups. I was crawling really fast. The preacher just kept looking up to the open ceiling over the pulpit and praying. Just as I got there crawling all the way because I didn't want anyone to see me, Mommy with my shoe in her hand swatted me on the butt with the shoe and holding on to me real tight like almost squeezing the breath out of me, she knelt down at the alter holding on to the shoe and me. The preacher I think said, "Hallelujah, Praise the Lord," and a whole lot of other things that I couldn't remember and a bunch of people came up to the alter and prayed that the Lord would forgive my Mother for her sins. They all cried and I did too because my Mommy had pinched me real hard a bunch of times while we were kneeling there being prayed for. Well I didn't get to see God but I sure didn't stop planning how I was going to. When I got home I got my butt swatted a few more times. It took a good while for the bruises to go away where Mommy pinched me. My daddy called them holy bruises. Some of the people at church talked about that and we all laughed. They asked me if I had seen god yet. I said, "No, but I'm still looking."

The black people were having church right across the road from the church we went to. They had school there too. When they had church, sometimes they would have dinner on the ground and singing and preaching all day. Some of the older kids from our church went over and were standing around looking in the windows. Their music was so good and they had really good singers. There were so many people there because they came from other places far away. Some of them had cars. Us kids wanted to go so bad and I guess Mommy had a moment of weakness for us so she said if you go you have to go right in the church and sit down and if there is no place to sit you go up front where the little kids are and sit on the floor. So she just took us over and walked right in with us. She stood at the back for a few minutes and one of the ladies that Mommy knew came over to her. Mommy had delivered all her babies and she liked her a lot. She told her we wanted to stay so there was no problem. The lady's name was Minnie and her husband was the preacher and his name was Sam. They lived not to far from us. Minnie just took us up front with the little kids and we sat on the floor. When the music would start we would clap our hands and sing when we knew the songs. It was the most fun we had since Daddy had died. We stayed the whole day and ate dinner there also. Sam and Minnie were in a wagon and they dropped us off on their way home. When we went in we could tell everyone was mad. Mommy didn't say much and Orme had been crying. I was sure it had something to do with us going to church, and not coming home with Mommy. We had such a good day and we had to pay a big price.

It was almost time for school to start and I was so excited and Bill was too. It was his first year but he knew a lot of things. He knew his numbers and ABC's. He could write his name and a whole lot of three letter words and a few four letter words. We had learned a lot of really bad words that we only used when we had free time, in the woods and the water.

School started earlier in our school in Kentucky than where Johnie was in Indiana. There was still a lot of work to be done. There were vegetables to harvest and can. Tobacco had to be worked in and the cane was almost ready to strip and cut for molasses. It was just too much. We were all just so tired all the time.

One morning at breakfast Robert wanted to talk. I knew it wasn't going to be good. He said, "Well, you know how much work there is to be done here and we've got a lot of mouths to feed. I think that it won't hurt Bert any to keep her out of school this year. She's pretty smart and already knows how to count the egg money and she can read a newspaper faster and better than me." He just sat there for a minute not saying anything just looking at me and I had begun to get mad and he looked at Bill and said; "Now its Bill's first year so he'll need to go so he can learn to read better and count. Now we'll just keep Bert home this year. She can go next year." He got up from the table and Mommy got up too and she picked up her chair and threw it across the kitchen floor. She said, "Bert will go to school and she'll go this year." Robert didn't know what to do or say. He picked up the chair and threw it back into the dining room, and said, "Let's get the work done." Mommy said, "You get the work done. Me and the kids are going to town."

Robert made Orme stay home that day. Mommy put a few things in an old hand bag for me and we walked over to the place where we sold separated cream and butter Mommy made, and the man who came to pick up the cream and butter gave us a ride to town in his truck. When we got to the bus station Mommy sat on the bench and wrote a letter and told me when I got to London give that to the Ticket Master. She put his name on the letter and said, "He is my first cousin and I've told him what to do. You'll stay all night with him and his family. He'll give you the tickets you need. And each time you change busses go to the Ticket Master and give him the envelope addressed to him. That's all you have to do. Now you are going to school and you're going to every year. You can't be held back. I won't let that happen."

I hated to leave Mommy and the boys and I dreaded the trip because I always got sick and I hadn't traveled on the bus or train all by myself before. I loved grandma and wanted to see Johnie so bad. I was so mixed up, I just wished Daddy hadn't died and we were all back together where we belonged.

It was almost time for the bus and I was heartsick. Mommy, Bill, Toots, and I all held on together and cried. Mommy told me she was going to give it a month and if things didn't get better she was leaving Robert. They sure couldn't get any worse but I didn't say that to Mommy.

I had a red crocheted hat on. I'll never forget it. Mommy had made it and starched it with what she called sugar starch and it was stiff as a board. You could knock someone out with it but it was pretty. I always liked a hat. Back then when women and girls dressed up they most always wore a hat and gloves too, even in hot weather. I didn't have gloves but I had that old hand bag with my letters and a few clothes and some crackers and a couple of apples. Mommy always remembered the train ride and the conductor that was so nice to us. I just can't imagine how sad and hurt Mommy was. She must have thought because Robert was well off and had a big house and land it would be a good thing to marry him. It didn't seem to be working out at all.

When the bus pulled up Mommy was right there as soon as the door was opened, talking to the bus driver. She asked him to let me sit close to him on one of the front seats and to be sure that he took me to the Station Master in London. When I got on the bus Toots and Bill were both crying. Toots was saying, "Don't go sissy," over and over again. I was trying not to cry but I couldn't help it. I didn't want everyone on the bus looking at me but I guess at the time they couldn't hardly help it. A little eight year old girl carrying an old worn hand bag that drug the ground and a red crocheted hat starched stiff as a board, and tears just rolling down my face which I had no control over at all. The driver put me in the seat right behind him. The bus wasn't crowed so I had the seat to myself. He told me I could lay down on the seat if I wanted to and he told me to use my hand bag for a pillow and that seemed like a good thing to me so that's what I did. I just stretched out on the seat and sat the hat on my face so no one could see me. I traveled all the way to London like that.

Mommy's cousin was right there when the bus stopped. He had the biggest smile on his face. I was the first one off the bus and he just picked me up and said, "I'd have known you anywhere. You look just like your mommy." He even kissed me on the check several times. He took me into the station and there was a place to eat. There was a counter the full length of the big building. There were stools you couldn't move, all the way down the counter and they turned around real easy. He sure didn't intend for any one to move them. He wanted to feed me right then but I told him I wasn't hungry and I would eat later. I sat my handbag down and got the letter I was supposed to give him and he read it right there. He kept looking at me every little bit.

All his family worked in the station. It wasn't just a bus station, it was a store too, and there were shelves and counters all over the place. They sold everything you could imagine there, tools, toys, feed, seed, groceries, material, cream separators, and sewing machines. Stuff was hanging on the walls and in barrels. It was just about the biggest store I had ever seen. He sold coal there. People would bring sacks and buy a sack of coal. He sold wagons, big wagons that horses pulled and sleds. You just couldn't even name all the things they had there. He had several kids and they all helped in the store. They laughed and talked a lot, and loud too. We walked out through the coal yard and where they kept the wagons and sleds and opened a door in a big tool fence and there was their house. It was bigger than Robert's house. They called the store, "The Station." They ate all their meals in the station. No one had a special time to eat, just when they were hungry. Their special food was soup and they had several big kettles of different soups on the warmer. You could smell the vegetable soup and the chili. I had never eaten chili but being a soup person I was interested in how he made that soup. I asked him if I could have just a little bit of each soup. He laughed and said, "I've heard you make soup. You want it all in the same bowl or each one in a separate bowl." There were always people in the station and he knew them all. His name was Frank. They were all watching us with the soup sampling. He sat me up on a stool and told me not to fall off. He brought a small bowl of every kind of soup he had for me to taste and everyone was watching. I had all these bowls around me with a different spoon in each bowl. I didn't know where to start. I guess that was my first introduction to a real soup maker and all the soups were good. My potato soup was better than his but his vegetable soup was so good and I liked it better than all the others. I asked him to tell me how he made it and he did. He said he would write it down but I told him to tell me, I would remember. I told him how I made my potato soup and I told him mine was much better than his. Our audience had grown quite a bit so he went into the kitchen and got a bowl of butter and a pitcher of cream and added it to the potato soup and I was telling him what to do and he did just like I said and I tasted it and told him to put more salt and pepper in it and he did that. After all of that we tasted it again. He gave all those people a sample and they all bought a big bowl of soup. I felt so important. He like my red hat and sent all the kids through the store to find a pair of red gloves for me. They couldn't find any but the next day when I got on the bus he handed me a pair of red gloves and said, "I hope they fit." He had fixed a letter for each place I had to stop and numbered them from one thru five and I had to give them in order. The family had picked out some things in the store and filled my handbag so full it was fat and would hardly close. They were such good people. Frank had a talk with the bus driver and just wouldn't stop and the driver told him he was going to be late and he understood what to do. He just pulled the handle on the door to close it and almost knocked Frank down. I just sat back and pulled my hat over my face and thought about the boys and Mommy, and once in awhile I thought about Orme. I had my crackers and apples and wasn't as sick as usual.

All the stops went really well and when I got to Indiana my uncle was right there waiting for me. I was hoping Johnie would be there but I would have to wait to see him. Since I had been to Indiana last my grandma and my uncles moved. They had rented a big farm in the bottoms and it was an adventure for me. My great-grandma was still living and I was glad to see her. She didn't go outside much but if someone walked with her she could go. She recognized me right away as Nellie and that was fine. My cousin, who was a girl, lived near by. She was a couple of years younger than me. We would walk Old Granny but Old Granny didn't talk much to my cousin and wouldn't let her hold her hand. She would let me feed her a few bites, but she wouldn't feed herself. If you put the spoon into her hand she wouldn't close her fingers on it. She would just let it drop. She still chewed gum but she couldn't unwrap it.

Grandma just worked all the time and she wanted me to sit with Old Granny. She told me that was more help to her than anything I could do. I still would do some things even though she didn't ask me. Johnie spent most of his time with the men on the farm. The work there was a lot different. They had big tractors and trucks so there was a limit to what little kids could do. Sometimes I just sat beside Old Granny when she would take a nap and watch her sleep. I would ask her things about when she was a little girl. She would talk real good some days but some other days she would hardly say anything. I would just go over and over the things she told me in my mind and pretend I was her hiding behind trees and bushes trying to steal things from gardens and off clothes lines like she did when they were walking from down south to Kentucky during the civil war. Old Granny didn't want to use the chamber pot that Grandma kept bedside so I took her to the outhouse because there was no inside plumbing in that house and I would set with her until she had finished. We used a catalog for wiping. I would take the thin pages and crumple them to soften them for her. She would talk and talk while she sat there. We spent a lot of time in the outhouse.

After awhile school started and we rode the bus but we had to walk down a lane as did a few other children and wait for the bus at the church. It was a long ride to school on a very crooked and winding road up hill almost all the way and by the time we got to school I was sick at my stomach. I stayed that way until noon and then we started the ride back home and by the time I got off the bus I was sick again. It was just so awful. I never ate lunch even though I had a good lunch. Finally Grandma found out about the crackers. She didn't normally keep crackers on hand but she bought them for my lunch and peanut butter and when I ate that I didn't get as sick.

But as always things changed really fast, Robert and Mommy showed up to take us back to Kentucky about a month after school started. Johnie wouldn't go. He just said no and meant it. I never had a choice. Robert said I wouldn't have to miss any school and he told me how Orme missed me and the little boys needed me. Johnie stayed with our uncle most of the time since their boys were just a little older than him and he liked being with them. He wouldn't even talk to Robert. I guess Robert realized that what he had said about our daddy could never be unsaid. I was so lonely for Bill, Toots, and Mommy that I just pretended nothing had been said and I would take this chance to see the boys because I knew it wouldn't last long and in no time at all I'd be back with Grandma and Johnie. Robert had hired someone to bring Mommy and him to get us. They had a big fancy car. They stayed about three days and then we left. I was sad to leave Johnie but I was glad to be going to see Bill and Toots. We just could never be together it seemed to me.

I remember saying goodbye to Old Granny. She was so frail and weak. When I went into the room she was lying down but she had her clothes on. She wanted to sit up because she thought I had come to take her to the toilet. She said, "You shore took your time. I've been waiting a long time." So I helped her to the toilet. We sat in the toilet and I tore out the thin pages from the catalog and crumpled them and she talked to me and called me Nellie and told me how she used to visit the Indians where they lived when she was a little girl. I told her I had to go but she was in no hurry. I helped her back into the house and she put her shawl around my shoulders and told me not to get a chill and then she took her little brown bag that she kept the treats grandma bought for her and gave that to me. I told her I would take just one thing but she insisted I take it all. Grandma was standing in the door way and she nodded to me to take it. Old Granny said, "I'm tired, help me lay down and tomorrow I'll teach you to weave. Cattie has my loom somewhere but she'll get it out tomorrow." I helped her lay down and took her shoes off. She went right to sleep. It was so sad. Grandma walked out to the car with me. I tried to give the little bag of treats to Grandma but she wouldn't take it and she told me to keep the shawl that Old Granny had put around my shoulders. She told me Old Granny wouldn't make it another year, Grandma was like my mommy, she knew things like that.

On our way back we only stopped to fill the car with gas and go to the bathroom. Once we stopped at a grocery store and Robert got some crackers, bologna, and cheese. They got some pop and moon pies also. Robert like those big old moon pies. Mommy and I sat in the back seat and she held my hand and talked to me. I thought that was about the best trip I had ever made and I had been on a few. She told me she and Robert had a long talk and he said if she wouldn't leave him he wouldn't keep us out of school and we wouldn't have to work so hard. He would hire some men to help more often.

I still got sick and boy was I ever sick now. Mommy had dropped off to sleep and I just lay down in the floorboard of the car. There were some coats and old clothes in the floorboard. I used them to make a sort of bed. The longer I lay there the sicker I got. Mommy was asleep and I could hear her making funny little noises as she got her breath. I didn't want to wake her up but I got sicker and I thought I was dying and I would just be real quiet and everyone would really be sorry when they tried to get me up and I would be all stiff and cold. I couldn't even die right because I started heaving so hard I threw up all over that pile of clothes. I made enough noise that the car stopped right there on the road. It was a good thing it was nighttime and the traffic wasn't heavy. The driver pulled off the road and everyone got out and helped me out of the car. What a mess, I was so sick I couldn't stand and had ruined that pile of clothes. Mommy cleaned me up and put clean clothes on me. The cold damp air made me feel so much better. The driver's name was Billy and he was related to Robert. He told Robert the gas fumes would have killed me if I hadn't gotten sick and that we should keep the windows open a little and I should ride in the front seat. When the seating arrangements were changed we headed onto Manchester. The trip seemed to take forever. The creeks weren't so full of water and Billy was able to drive across the creek where the water was shallow and we didn't have to walk across the footbridge. Bill and Toots were standing on the footbridge waiting. I like to think they were waiting just for me and they ran along beside the car until we got to the house. We hugged each other and danced around and ran away to hide and just be little kids.

I told them all about Johnie and the school and how awful the ride on the school bus was. They asked so many questions. I gave them the bag of goodies Old Granny had given to me before we left Indiana. We weren't used to having candy and gum very often and the boys made short work of that. I didn't eat any of it and told them I had that kind of stuff all the time at Grandma's.

We went to school the next day. Toots went along with us even though he was just four. He didn't do anything. Just hung around the school yard and at recess he would play with the kids. No one bothered him. He could play all the games the other kids played. He wouldn't come in the school during class time but he would hang around the store, which was across the road from the school. When school was out he would be there waiting for us. There were no busses and everyone had to walk to school. The school was about two miles from where we lived. It didn't seem to bother Toots to walk back and forth to school. He just had fun no matter what he did. He would walk with one foot in the rut, splashing the water out. If he wore shoes it made no difference. He picked up rocks and threw them at whatever struck his fancy. We all threw rocks on the two mile walk. There were rocks, which were better to throw and hit the target easier. Bill and Toots always carried several in their pockets just in case they needed them. School was going pretty good and we were learning a lot. There was also a lot of work to do when we got home and so there wasn't hardly any let up at all.

That year we all went to the fair and Robert took his mules and entered them in a pulling contest. We were all excited about the rides and animals and games. We had never been to a fair before. Robert's mules won the first prize. It was like a party at home that night. The next morning even before we were out of bed we were woke up by a car horn blowing in the yard. It was one of Mommy's brothers to tell us Old Granny had died. Mommy and Robert got ready and went to Indiana with my uncle. We kids stayed home with Orme. I don't really know what I felt. I was sad but I didn't want to go to the funeral. I just didn't want to see Old Granny dead. I knew what dead looked like.

When Mommy and Robert came back they had Johnie with them. We were so happy to see him. I never knew what they told him to get him to come home with them but it was the best thing that had happened to us for a long time. He was bigger and had learned a lot of things. We laughed at him because he talked different from us. We called it talking proper. When he would say, "Hi," we always said, "Howdy." We laughed at his, "Hi."

Johnie went to school with us and on our way to school we found a nest where the old hen had hid out and laid some eggs. It was by the foot of the footbridge down by the mill. We walked by it everyday on our way to school. There were several eggs in it and we had quite a talk about whether we should tell Mommy or just use the eggs ourselves. Johnie told us he could eat an egg raw. We dared him and he did, but he gagged and we laughed at him for a while and then I decided we should divide them or buy pop or candy and crackers with the money. The candy and pop won out. After the first trip to the store we had to wait a week and half before we got enough eggs for candy and pop again.

We fed that old hen really good. It was beginning to get cold at night and Robert and Mommy had begun to talk about stripping tobacco. We weren't looking forward to that. We knew we would have to miss some school for that. We talked a lot about stripping tobacco. Toots was still going along with us to school. Bill was really smart but he didn't talk a lot. Sometimes he would stutter when he talked, not really bad. There was one kid at school who could hardly talk at all. He just opened his mouth and never says anything you could understand. That particular day when the first grade had their spelling class, each kid stood up one at a time and spelled the word the teacher gave him out loud before the whole school. Bill stuttered just a little but he spelled the word and you could understand him just fine. The teacher called him by the boy's name who stuttered really bad and the rest of the kids laughed. Johnie and I didn't laugh and Bill didn't either and without stuttering a bit he said, "You old son-of-a-bitch." Well there wasn't anyone laughing and Bill ran out of the room with the teacher right behind him and Johnie and I right behind her. She was aiming to whip him for sure. Toots showed up and Johnie yelled, "Get some rocks," Bill, Toots, and I started gathering rocks for Johnie to throw. There was nothing she could do but retreat, and we went home. Boy I tell you, Mommy was mad as an old wet hen. We were all talking at once and finally told her what happened. Robert wasn't home and we were all glad of that. When he got home Mommy told him what had happened. He was fit to be tied and we thought he was going to beat us to death. He surly didn't believe us. The next morning Mommy took us to school and she talked to the teacher who didn't see anything wrong with calling Bill by the other boy's name. Mommy wrote a letter to the school superintendent who came out and talked to Mommy and Robert. We got out of school for a whole week and when we went back we had a new teacher.

Things weren't so smooth at home. Robert was all ready to whip us all. There wasn't much talking at mealtime and it was hard for us to set at the table because Robert always wanted to talk at mealtime and insisted that everyone join in. He was a real storyteller and always managed to include everyone in the conversation. That morning he wanted to talk about politics and some stories that were on the front page of the newspaper. Robert and I were the only ones who read all the paper. He wanted to talk about why I read the paper and why everyone else read it. Well, that was no fun, because Mommy never had time and she told him so. The boys in turn read the funnies or just looked at them. After Mommy's short answer he asked me and I told him I was looking for news about Miss Linda and that's why I read it all. Once in awhile there would be something about her in the social pages and sometimes on the front page but you had to read it all. When he got to Bill, Bill began to stutter because he was scared and excited and he couldn't say a thing. Robert just turned around to Mommy and said, "See what that teacher had to put up with." Well he sure said the wrong thing then because Mommy jumped up and grabbed the tablecloth and pulled it off the table with everything that was on it. Boy that was some mess. He hit her really hard and they hit each other. We kids were screaming and Mommy's face was bleeding. Robert was trying to stop her but she was going to fight to the death. Orme had already gone to work so she wasn't there. There was no work done that day by us. Mommy just got a few things together and cleaned us kids up and we started walking to town and on our way to Grandma's again. Before we left he managed to get me alone and gave me two twenty dollar bills and said to hide the money until Mommy had cooled down and then give it to her. He showed me how to stick it down into my sock and keep it hid. I think looking back that was one of the heaviest loads I've carried ever but I managed to carry it all the way to Indiana. Thank God for Grandmas.

Charity, Bert, Bill, & Toots

Chapter 9
The End of Time

I don't think I was ever at Grandma's house when she didn't have visitors. There weren't enough beds so she fixed us kids a bed on the floor. We didn't mind because we were so tired from the trip. We took our coats and shoes off and slept in our clothes. I had forgotten all about the money and sometime through the night I took my socks off and the money was in them.

When we woke up the next morning Mommy and Grandma were folding the quilts and found the money. I was the only one who knew about the money and I wasn't telling. Mommy began to threaten Johnie because she thought he had taken it from someone. I had to tell her. I couldn't let Johnie take the blame. It seemed as if there was a crisis everyday that had to be cried about. When one of us kids cried, we all cried. Johnie did what he always did, just turned around and walked off.

Mommy's younger brother was mad because we had come to Grandma's again. He told everyone he hated it when Mommy and Robert had a spat and she came to Grandma's. Mommy just asked one of her cousins to take her to an older brother who lived farther away. He welcomed us. He knew what a hard time Mommy was having and her face looked so bad where Robert had hit her. He told her the younger brother was hot headed and not to pay him no mind, that he didn't like any kids. I thought Robert must have been like that when he was young. My uncle had two girls close to my age and I liked them a lot. They didn't have to work like we did. They were so good to us. There was a family that lived near them who had some boys about the same age as Bill and Toots. We all had such a real good fun time. We just pretended to be regular kids.

One morning right after breakfast a big car pulled up. It was Robert and his nephew. His nephew was driving the car. He had red hair and his name was Robert. Everyone called him Red Bob. I knew mommy didn't want to be at Grandma's or anywhere in Indiana, and I knew she would go back to Kentucky. She tried to talk Johnie into going back with us. He said he couldn't ride that far in the same car with Robert so he stayed in Indiana. I don't know what I felt; all I had ever wanted was to be with my whole family. I also knew that would never happen again. On the way back I didn't eat anything. I tried to sleep and to keep from eating and being sick. I just thought I would never get over being car sick.

Orme was excited to see us. She hugged us all and fixed us something to eat. We had only missed a few days of school. Mommy and Robert were talking about some timber he had sold to someone. It was a big job and he was going to hire some people to help if he could find them. He had to cut the trees, get them out of the woods and down to the mill. Then he had to saw them into lumber. He called it a house pattern. He knew all about how to figure how much lumber to saw and how long to make the boards. You could give him a picture or a blue print and he could figure everything you would need to build it. He was a smart man. He was smart as he was mean.

We had a grist mill but we only ground meal and wheat flour one Saturday a month. That was always like a holiday because people would bring a wagon with their grain in it and their whole families. Robert had two rental houses on his place and the men were usually glad to help him to make some extra money or pay their rent. Coal mining was about all the work available for men around there.

He knew of a black family that had moved near by so he hired that man. The man told him he had two kids and his wife was sickly. He would have to bring the kids with him to work. They were my age, a boy and a girl. Robert agreed to let him bring them if they wouldn't get in the way. The boy was bigger than me so Robert said he could do a few things at the mill. The little girl hung out with me and I loved it. She would help me do things. I just loved her. One day Robert came up to the house to get something and we were in the house. Robert didn't like black people at all but he needed help so bad. When he saw her in the house with me he got so mad and I thought he was going to beat me to death. He said so many bad things to me. His old mean words were worse than any whipping he could ever give me. After he was through cussing me out he began on my new little friend. He told her he didn't allow n****s in his house playing with his kids. I was crying and hugging her and she was crying too. We didn't know what we had done. The little girl's dad quit right away and took his kids home, and again I wasn't talking to Robert. The black family moved away and I didn't see them again.

Right after that there was a death in Robert's family. It was a cousin of his and a lot of people came from out of state and stayed about three days. We had to do a lot of cooking and fixing places for them to sleep. Orme took off from work and Mommy had to stay at the house to fix food and see to the company. She couldn't help with the chores or go to the mill like she always did. The women visitors pitched in and helped do a lot of things. I was on vacation. I did a real good job of being invisible.

Women back then didn't talk about sex or tell their kids about personal things about how their bodies changed or where babies came from. Now this bunch of women was different. They were from the city and some of them smoked cigarettes and would join in on a drink of moonshine. Some used bad words and didn't think a thing about it. They wore high heeled shoes and silk stockings and lots of lipstick and rouge. You wouldn't think they had come to a funeral.

At meal time there wasn't enough room for everyone to eat at once. Robert made make shift tables with saw horses and lumber but there still wasn't enough room. The men and older women would eat first. The younger women and kids ate last. After the meal was over the men and older people went out on the porch and talked. The younger women sat around in the dining room and drank coffee and tea and talked about different things. The visitors were interested in Mommy being a midwife. They were asking her all kinds of questions, like how many babies she had delivered and who the mothers were. One asked her if she delivered any black babies. Mommy said she helped anyone who needed her. I was trying to be invisible so I curled up under the table and pretended to be asleep. Then they asked about one lady that wasn't married. Mommy told them she had delivered that baby. The next question was is it a boy or girl? Then they asked was it mixed? Well, Mommy said it was white as you or me, but yes it was mixed. Then they wanted to know how you could tell? Mommy thought a little before she answered. I could tell she was getting tired of that subject but she told them if it was mixed its private parts would be just as black as could be.

Well now how about that! I had a plan. They wouldn't let me drink coffee because it would turn you black. I always liked coffee. So my plan was to drink all the coffee I could because I wanted to turn black. I would see what Robert will do about that, when I turned black. I began by drinking all the coffee anyone left in cups. I didn't care who I was drinking after. It was easy because I washed almost all the dishes. I even emptied the coffee pot. When the funeral was over and everyone had gone home, well almost everyone, Roberts's older sister decided she wanted to stay awhile, that didn't stop my plan; I just kept drinking the left over coffee, and draining the pot. After about a week I checked myself. I had a hand mirror and I laid it on the floor and squatted down over it and took a look. I wasn't black yet. We had a coffee grinder on the wall. We bought coffee beans and ground them, so I began eating the grounds. Now that was awful, so I changed that and started eating the whole beans. That was pretty good; they were crunchy and kind of like nuts. So I began checking myself everyday but it wasn't working at all. I kept trying. My patience was running out and I was running around like a dog chasing its tail. It wasn't working at all and I was feeling like a loser. I had been set on turning black.

Robert's old sister was driving us all crazy, especially me. With Robert and Mommy out in the woods and at the mill so much trying to get the trees cut and the belts changed on the mill and Orme working at the store, us kids were pretty much on our own. Mommy was trying to figure out what was wrong with me. She threatened to take me to the doctor. I hardly slept at all and was running around and jumping at every little noise. Orme figured out what I was doing with the coffee thing. She said if I didn't stop she was going to tell on me. She said people drank coffee to keep them awake. She told me that was why we had that big coffee pot we hardly ever used only when there was a funeral or some one was bad sick and people had to stay awake a long time. I took one more look at my bottom and quit but I kept a few beans in my pocket for emergences.

Robert's old sister took on the job of managing us kids. She was worse than Robert. We did a lot of the chores and she didn't like the way we did anything. She was worse on me because what I did most was in the house. She sat about trying to teach me the right way to do everything. It didn't take me long to say I don't know how, show me.

I would step back and watch. That didn't work long. I wasn't doing anything but watching, and nothing was getting done. She told on me. I tried to cry but I didn't mean it. I was still jumping around from the coffee fix. I told Robert the only thing that was wrong with me was his mean old sister. Well, I lied out of that one. I wasn't afraid of her but I was afraid God would do something to me for lying.

The very next day old sister decided us kids should trim the grass around the house. Robert cut it with the big hay mower every now and then but old sister got Mommy's scissors and butcher knives and told us to trim the grass. When Robert and Mommy came up from the mill, we were on our knees crawling around with scissors and knives cutting grass. Mommy wanted to know what was going on. Robert didn't say anything. He just took his hat off and began hitting it against his leg real hard. That is what he did when he got real mad. Mommy was gathering up her scissors and knives and examining them. Robert told old sister that the grass was his job and it wasn't changing.

Orme had to leave for work early the next morning but she helped me do the dishes before she left. Mommy and Robert had already left for the mill. Old sister was just getting up. We kids were getting ready to leave for school. Old sister decided I should make the beds before I left. She told the boys to go ahead; I could catch up with them. There were four beds to be made and they were feather beds. That was a crying job, but I half way made them up. By the time I left the boys were well out of sight. When I got to the fork in the road I saw one of the bigger school boys coming down that road. He saw me and began to run. I was afraid of him and I began to run faster and he did too. Now I'm crying and he is gaining on me. When I looked back he was unbuttoning his pants. I thought he was going to pee and I kept running and he did too. I'm running as fast as I can and I saw the school. He began to slow down. Bill must have told the teacher I was going to be late because she was out watching for me. I lost my power and just fell at her feet. I told her about the boy and she sent him home. The teacher went to the boy's home and told his folks about what happened. They took their kids out of the school. When Mommy found out about old sister making me late for school she insisted old sister leave. Robert was alright with that. I always thought I would have never been able to out run that boy if I hadn't been eating the coffee beans. Back then little kids didn't walk to school alone. Some bad things had happened to kids walking by themselves.

Things began to settle down a little and one evening late just before dark the sky began to light up in the North. It wasn't lightening. It was huge bands of colors just rolling all around. There was every color you could name and some times the red color would look like fire. Everyone at the mill was just getting ready to go home and even the grown men were scared. They all thought it was the end of the world. Some of them just fell down on their knees and started praying. Robert's son-in-law was there and he got his little Bible out and began trying to find the chapter that told what the end would look like. I knew Robert was smart as he was mean and I just stood and watched everything he did. I wasn't going to move from where I was standing until he did. He turned around a couple of times and looked at everyone and took his hat off and hit it against his leg a few times and announced that he better get the creek banks cleaned off and he would have to work on the mowing machine. He looked at his son-in-law, who was trying to get on his mule. He spent more time on the ground. Robert hitched up his mules to the wagon and tied Joe's mule to the wagon and loaded him up and took him home. The next day there was no school. No one came to work at the mill. Robert said we would have two weeks and there would be a baptism. Everyone and his uncle would join the church on Sunday and the next Sunday would be the baptism. So we might as well start getting ready.

Some of the people came to their senses and tried to do what they had to do. But Robert's son-in-law had a hard time. He just couldn't start his life like it was before the big light show. He would sit and read the Bible all day long. His wife fed him, dressed him and put him to bed. The doctor said he would come around but it would take a while. The doctor was right half way. His wife waited on him hand and foot the rest of his life. He would sit in a rocking chair and read the Bible.

Old sister's daughter came and took her home. We were glad to see her go and I think she was glad to go. We were just about ready for the big day. We had cut weeds, picked up rocks, trimmed willow branches away from the creek banks and Robert had dragged gravel out of the creek to make the water deeper. He fixed the mowing machine and mowed the grass. Everything looked so good.

Uncle John heard about the baptism and he came over and brought some moonshine in fruit jars. That was a must for an event of that size. Robert hid it but everyone knew there was some around some place. Uncle John never came around without bringing something for us kids. This time he brought pocket knives for the boys and he brought a little black curly haired dog for me. Its name was Maggie. I was so excited. Robert didn't like that one bit. He said, "Take that back with you." Uncle John said, "Now Rob, you don't mean that. Tell you what I'll do. Let her keep the dog and I'll give you the shine half price." Robert agreed but he gave me a long talk about having a dog. It's a no good dog. It's not a working dog. It's a waste of time. It can't go in the house. It can't bark. It can't go to the barn or the mill. It's trouble on four feet and he changed its name to trouble.

A few days before the baptism, Maggie began to scoot around on her behind. She would scoot all over the place and Mommy said she had worms and we would have to put turpentine on her behind. Mommy got the bottle and started out to put it on her and Robert said, "That's

Bert's dog let Bert take care of her dog." So Mommy handed the bottle to me and said Robert is right, and I took it. I didn't know what I was doing so I caught her but I couldn't hold on to her. Toots went in the house and got a chicken leg with a little meat on it so while she was eating the chicken leg; I poured the whole bottle on her. She jumped up and began to run as hard as she could into the creek. All three of us right behind her. We thought she would drown. She went right into the deep part where Robert had drug out the gravel to make it deeper. We were all over our heads but we could swim. Maggie could swim faster. We finally got her headed toward the shallow part. We were headed down the creek away from the house toward the mill. We weren't aware of it but we just put a show on that made everyone laugh till they cried. We were a good ways from the house and Robert yelled at us. He said, "Reckon you kids could do that again Sunday for the baptism."

There weren't many church houses around back then. There was a Presbyterian church about one and half miles from our house thanks to Robert. He never went much but he knew how to build churches too. The other dominations used school houses or some met in their homes. Black people didn't mix with whites and they used their school houses. There were two groups of Baptists and three groups of Holy Rollers. There were plenty of places they could have used to baptize in, but Robert always cleaned up around the creek and it was easy to get to so all the preachers close around brought their new members to our creek to be baptized. Plus there was always that drink the men folk knew Robert would have.

The day before the big event while we were eating breakfast, Robert and Mommy talked about what roll us kids would play on the big day. We were excited but scared too. Robert said they could go to the barn and play and take some food and have a picnic. We would have to tie up trouble. Mommy said let the boys go the barn. They could play ball or tag and the girls could stay at the house and act like girls. So that's the way it was except Maggie could be locked up in the crib and there wasn't anything I could do about that. There would be some big boys and they weren't very nice sometimes and they talked really bad.

Sunday morning came sooner than I wanted. I went straight to the barn as soon as I finished my chores to see about Maggie. She was alright. I was the only one that called her Maggie. Everyone else called her Trouble. Mommy and Orme were busy making coffee and tea. They used the funeral pot. We didn't fix food for the crowd. They always had dinner at their church before the baptism, but just in case someone got hungry Mommy made a big kettle of vegetable soup. And a whole bunch of corn bread muffins, and two big cobblers.

People began to come in wagons. There was a wagon full after wagon full. The boys were glad to go to the barn. They came prepared with balls and bats. The girls were glad to watch the goings on at the baptism. The men used the mill house for a changing room and the women used the house. We had two big toll boxes in the mill house, one for corn and one for wheat. That was where Robert hid the moonshine. He put the fruit jars down under the grain.

I was having a real hard time staying away from the barn. There were those mean boys and no telling what they would do to Maggie.

There were singers from all the different groups. They all took turns singing. They stood down on the creek bank and each group sang two songs and after they had finished they all sang together and then everybody sang. It sounded so good. The Holy Rollers sang the loudest and when they prayed you couldn't understand a thing they said. The Baptist preachers prayed the longest. The Presbyterians were the quietest but they were the best sounding singers. I don't know how many were baptized that day but it was a lot. Some of them were really big and it took two and sometimes three preachers to lift them out of the water. They dropped one big person and the preachers had to go under the water to get her out. Everyone laughed. There was so much going on at the swimming hole, no one was watching what was going on at the barn.

The first thing the boys did was let Maggie out of the corn crib. She loved to play ball. If the boys didn't catch the ball she got it. Then they had to chase her down to get the ball. They had a real good game going. One hit the ball into the pig pen. There were twenty pigs in there that weighed about one hundred pounds each. So naturally Maggie had to get that ball. But first of all she had to chase a few pigs. That was when all Hell broke loose. Here came twenty pigs, one dog and about two dozen boys out of the hollow, down the branch that ran into the swimming hole where the baptism was just winding down.

Maggie was having the time of her life. I wanted to help so badly. I don't know what the plan was but it wasn't working. All the wet people and a few brave dry ones got into the act. All the dry ones were cheering the wet ones and the animals on. It took a while to get the pigs turned around back to the barn. What a good time everyone had. Everyone forgot about the end of time and why they were getting baptized. It was almost dark when everyone left. I managed to stay out of Roberts's way for the rest of that day. Mommy didn't have to worry about all that food. It was gone real fast.

The next day when I got home from school I couldn't find Maggie anywhere. Mommy came up from the mill and made me help her in the kitchen. When they worked at the mill and we went to school the dinner dishes were left and that was my job to wash and help get supper. I had wasted a lot of time looking for Maggie. Mommy said not to worry because dogs were like that. They wander off and hunt rabbits and chase all kind of things. She'll be back. She didn't come home that night or the next day. The boys helped me hunt for her but it was no use. About a whole week went by and one of the men that worked at the mill came up to the house and told us he had found her. Someone had killed her, shot her right in the head. He said he wasn't going to tell us and then he saw us hunting and calling for her and had to tell us. He said he buried her and he showed us where he buried her. No one knew who killed her. Robert hated her and I thought he killed her. Orme tired to comfort me, she didn't think Robert killed her but she couldn't change my mind.

Chapter 10
Back to Indiana

About two weeks went by and it was Saturday. Orme worked late on Saturday and it was dark when she came home. She had to walk home from the church where she parked the car. The road was bad. The walk was about one mile and a half. That night when she came in she was crying and her clothes were torn and she had blood on her and the flashlight. We were all around her. She said someone had attacked her. She hit him a whole bunch of times with her flashlight. She said he had been drinking because she could smell him. She said he was in worse shape than she was. That he had fell down the road bank and down a hill so she ran. Boy that made Robert mad. He got his gun and went on the hunt. He didn't find him. If he had he would have killed whoever it was.

I was still moping around over Maggie. I would always believe Robert killed her. Mommy began watching me more than usual. I'm not talking to Robert at all, as usual. Another week went by and Mommy's older brother came to see us and Mommy packed some clothes for me. Mommy and Robert told me I had to go stay with Grandma for a while because they were afraid the person that tried to hurt Orme would come back and get after me. I wasn't big enough or strong enough to fight him off and I might get hurt real bad. So one more time I headed back to Grandma. I loved Grandma but I sure didn't want to leave Bill and Toots, but I would get to see Johnie. I think I had changed a lot for I knew in my heart that day I didn't belong anywhere and I was so sad.

It was a long trip. My uncle had some people with him and they kept stopping and buying food to snack on. I knew if I ate anything I would throw up. They kept trying to get me to eat something. The very smell of the stuff made me sick. It was the longest trip ever.

Going to school at Grandma's wasn't easy. There were several kids there that were from Kentucky like me. The Indiana kids acted like they were better than us. They had better clothes than us and even the food we ate was funny to them. The teacher didn't believe I was in the grade I said I was and I had to take a big bunch of tests. He didn't believe I was eleven years old so he went to Grandma's and asked her all kinds of questions about me. He wasn't a very nice man. Johnie was there and he helped me out a lot. He didn't stay at Grandma's. He stayed with Mommy's older brother who had kids close to his age. They watched out for him.

Right around Christmas time I began to have headaches and felt sick a lot. I didn't tell Grandma. She had some cures and I knew she would try them on me and I knew I didn't want them. One morning I woke up early and my bed was wet. I didn't wet the bed. I felt the bed with my hand and it was wet and sticky and red. It was blood. I was scared. I knew I had done a few things and told a few lies and promised God I'd do some things I didn't get done but I thought he would give me some time to make up for them. I didn't want to die. I just covered up my head and lay there and cried. I was afraid to make any more promises I couldn't keep. It would probably be better for everyone if I just laid there and bled to death.

Then Grandma came in to wake me up. She said, "Honey ain't you going to go to school?" I told her no, I am dying. I'm bleeding to death.

I wasn't very big for my age, but she just picked me up covers and all and sat in the big rocking chair and rocked me for a while. Then she told me all about how a little girl became a woman. I would have rather died. I was mad at Mommy for not telling me what was going to happen to me. I wondered why she didn't throw me in the swimming hole and drown me when I was a baby, like Sissy did when she found her baby. Grandma kept me out of school the rest of the week. I followed her around asking her all kinds of questions. She tried to answer them and told me a lot of things I didn't ask for. Grandma sent my aunt to town to get me some new underwear and pads, which I hated but I had to get used to them if I was going to live.

At Grandma's she never told me what to do. If my clothes needed washing I washed them, or mended I did that too. If not I wore them like they were. I helped my aunt Bertha strip tobacco on the weekends and she paid me. She would let me use her sewing machine and show me how to sew some things. She said it was her job to help me because I was her name sake. I guess I had grown up a little like Grandma said I would.

I wasn't very popular at school. I would go to Grandma's to school a while and then back to Kentucky and back to Grandma's. I just never got to make friends. I didn't stay anywhere long enough.

As soon as school was out, Mommy sent money for bus tickets for me to come home. This time I didn't want to go home but I had the trip all figured out and didn't need anyone to help me. When I finally got off the bus in Manchester I went to the store where Orme worked and rode home with her. She was surprised at how much I had grown. I didn't seem to fit in anymore. I had grown up and the boys had too. We didn't know what to say to each other. I was washing dishes and Toots was standing there watching me. I turned around real fast and said, Boo! He jumped like I had shot him. We both laughed and I told him if he would stick around till I got done we would walk over to Maggie's grave and clear around it. Bill went with us. There was a little woods there and moss had grown on the stones. We pulled the weeds around and found some more stones and arranged them all around. We picked wild flowers and put them on the grave also. We talked about Maggie and how big she would have been if she had lived. We figured she would have pups by this time and we made up names for them. We talked about the cuss words we made up and laughed at that. I asked them if they thought Robert and Mommy would be mad if we went to Daddy's grave. It wasn't far. It was about as far as the school house. I told them if Robert and Mommy got mad I would tell them I made you boys go with me. I didn't care what they did to me. I bet I wouldn't cry. I would just smile at them. So we took off and picked everything that had a bloom on it along the road sides. We talked about the last time we went to Daddy's grave. We got punished pretty good for that and it didn't kill us. This time no one even missed us, or asked us what we did.

It was peach canning time in Kentucky. There was a truck that came up from Georgia every year and sold peaches to the people in our county. We always bought several bushels. Mommy began telling me what she wanted me to do that day to get ready for the canning. Just like any grown up would have done at that time, I said I can't work in the peaches. I've started my period today. I thought Mommy would have a heart attack. She said one word, "When?" I said, "Right before my birthday, and thanks for telling me about all that stuff." I was twelve years old that year and they didn't send me away.

There were brand new teachers who had been to college that year. Usually the teachers would be just out of high school. These teachers were young and were married to each other. They took an interest in me for some reason. I thought it was because I was a loner. There was a war going on then and a lot of the young men joined the service.

There was also a draft, if you were over eighteen you were drafted. It was mandatory. Our teacher was drafted but when he went to be examined he had a health problem and they wouldn't take him. I was happy about that.

People were gathering junk metal for the war effort and the county was giving prizes to the schools for gathering junk. The parents would bring it to school in wagons and big trucks would come and take it to be melted down and made into vehicles or whatever was needed. The prizes were books for a library. They weren't new books but they all had the backs on them and all the pages. I thought that was the best thing ever. The teacher let me write the name of the school in every book. I felt real important. That was the best year of school I ever had. I read every one of those books.

That year Mommy showed me how to cut out a dress pattern. I helped make quilts. I could not believe how much my life had changed. It didn't bother me one bit that I had no close friends.

I was in the eighth grade. I wanted to go to Brea School which was in London Kentucky. You could live there and work your way through school. It didn't cost as long as you kept your grades and did the work assigned to you. The high school in our county was over ten miles from us and we had no school busses. Mommy wanted me to go but Robert said it was a waste of money and I needed to stay there to help do the work. He said I was smart enough. They had a big quarrel and didn't ask my opinion at all. I walked between them and said I'll fix this for you. I'll go back to Indiana and I won't ever come back here. They stopped yelling and I went on with my chores.

Every time I had any time for myself I began sorting out things I was going to take with me. It didn't take long because I had grown so much there wasn't a lot of stuff I could wear. School was out and it was the busiest time of the year. It was time to make tobacco beds and the garden had to be planted. The barn had to be cleaned out, and there was always the mill. Saturdays were grist mill day. Mommy needed some seed and onion sets, so she sent me to the store. The store that had seeds was pretty far away, but there was a short cut that in good weather could cut the trip in half. I knew how to go that way so she gave me the money and fifty cents for myself. I was glad to go.

It was a big woods. The trees were big but there was what they called a log trail so all you had to do was stay on the trail. About half way there I saw smoke a little off the trail, so I followed the smoke. There was Uncle John and his two nephews. I knew them all. Uncle John was working a still making moonshine. He began telling me about how dangerous it was for me to be walking by myself. I sat down and talked with him. I liked talking to Uncle John. He acted like I knew something. I told him all about how sad I was and that I was going to run away to Grandma's. He asked if I was going to walk all the way. I told him, yes if I had to. I told him I was saving my money and I had three dollars and I was going to save the fifty cents Mommy had given me to spend. They were all three listening to me without saying anything. Then he asked, what are you going to do when you get there. I told I was going to go school and be a teacher and never come back to Kentucky. He took a little book about the size of a deck of cards out of his pocket. He said your Daddy would never forgive me if I didn't help you out but you have to swear on this Bible that you won't ever tell anyone where you got this money to get to Indiana. I was crying and said that ain't a Bible. He said if we believe it's a Bible it's a Bible. I swore on that little book and took the money Uncle John and the boys gave me. Now I wouldn't have to wait and miss a lot of school.

I got to the store and gave the store keeper my list. There was an old man sitting on the bench eating something out of a box. "You ever tasted this?" he asked. I told him no. He held out the box to me and I took a hand full. It was so good. He said, "Them's corn flakes." I asked how much they cost. He told me twelve cents. So since I had some more money I decided to buy me a box. I ate most of them on the way home but saved some for Bill and Toots. I didn't tell them I was leaving. I thought I would wait until I was leaving and tell them then.

We were working planting the garden and a big car pulled up. It was Mommy's two older brothers. They had come to tell Mommy her youngest brother had been killed in a car wreck. He was coming home from Charleston powder plant where he worked and had a wreck that killed him instantly. Mommy and Robert got ready and went to Indiana with them. That left us kids and Orme to take care of everything while they were gone. Orme took off from work. We did a lot of things and had such a good time. We cooked the things we liked the very best. We laughed and sang. We acted like we were someone else and let the others try to guess who it was. That was so much fun. I was still putting things into the coffee sack I had under the bed planning to leave. We had planted a lot of the garden and done the washing and ironing. We had such a good time while Mommy and Robert were gone I was beginning to have second thoughts. But then I thought if my uncles brought them back I was going to just get in the car and go.

Sure enough Mommy's brothers brought them back. Orme came to me and told me I was doing the right thing. She said there was no way I would ever get to go to school if I stayed here. They were leaving the next day and I had my stuff all ready. I picked up my sack, put it in the car and climbed in. Orme had given me some money to go with what I had and told me to get just what I needed and it would last a long time. Mommy came running out to the car and asked, "What are you doing?" I just said I'm going to school. She hugged me and said be careful. I was thirteen years old.

Grandma was so sad. I was sad for her. She told me she lost her husband and four children to TB but she had been able to take care of them as long as they lived, with her youngest son she didn't even get to give him a drink of water. It was the worst thing of her life and she couldn't get over it.

I knew I was on my own, and that money wasn't going to last me forever but the farming was different in Indiana. We raised big gardens in Kentucky but here in Indiana they raised acres and acres of vegetables. The canning factories bought them. The farmers hired school kids to pick their vegetables. So I did that until school started. I was able to buy my books, shoes, a coat, and some sweaters. I didn't have to ask for money. Johnie was in the same grade as I was. He had missed a lot of school and I had caught up with him. I loved going to high school, but Johnie said he was going to quit. He would be sixteen in January. He would ride the bus to school in the morning and noon he would go to the pool room and play pool the rest of the day. When my aunt came through town from work at the powder plant he would ride home with her. He got to know some people who trimmed trees and weeds under power lines. They worked all over the State of Indiana. He played pool with them. They offered him a job with them and he took it. So he became a tree trimmer.

Mommy sent me some new dresses she made for me. They were so pretty. She was a real good hand to sew. She knew what was pretty for school girls and I could wear a different dress every day for seven days any how. There were a few boys who noticed me at school, but non I cared about. Most all the girls had a boyfriend.

Sometimes Grandma would get a ride to town on Saturday night. That was the big day. The stores stayed open as long as there was anyone there to buy stuff. Every Saturday was like Christmas on the square. There was plenty of money because the factories were making things for the war. There were always soldiers looking for girlfriends. People would walk around the square. Sometimes they would hold hands when they walked. Maybe they would stop and buy a drink or sandwich. That was big time. I was walking with a girlfriend and we run into a couple of boys we went to school with. They were just standing talking to a boy who was sitting in his car. One of the boys wanted to walk with me. The boy in the car kept looking at me like he had never seen a girl before. I knew I had never seen anyone that was as good looking as him. I was speechless but he wasn't. He said something that I didn't understand. Then he said, "I'm not much on walking but I sure would love to take you for a ride. Well that ride lasted fifty seven years and took my education plan in a whole new direction.

Bert & Victor wedding picture